THE IVF DAD

What I Learned On My Infertility Journey, and How It Can Help You

KEEGAN E. PRUE

Moving Forward Press

Keegan E. Prue

Printed in the United States of America
First Printing 2022
First Edition 2022

10 9 8 7 6 5 4 3 2 1

Disclaimers

The contents of this book are based on my years-long, often painful, yet sporadically humorous, experience with infertility during which I learned more about human reproduction than I ever intended. I have made every effort to ensure the information is accurate as of the time of publishing. However, this book is neither intended to be, nor should it be used as, a substitute for the medical advice of a licensed physician. Consult with a doctor in any matters relating to your health and/or the health of your partner.

Other than the names of the author and his immediate family, the names of all other people, companies, organizations, institutions, locations, and other entities have been changed to protect their identity and privacy.

For Olivia. I couldn't have done any of this without you. I appreciate everything you do for me and our family each and every day.

And for the staff of Boston IVF - Albany. You made our dreams come true.

TABLE OF CONTENTS

Welcome Note From the IVF DAD 1
Introduction 3
Chapter 1 15
Step One is Accepting: When "Trying" isn't "Working"
Chapter 2 35
A Chapter About Feelings
Chapter 3 59
Four Factors to Help You Choose a Clinic
Chapter 4 73
Potential Diagnoses: What's the Root Cause?
Chapter 5 89
Potential Treatments
Chapter 6 113
Navigating the Ups and Downs of Treatment
Chapter 7 141
When Things Go Wrong
Chapter 8 159
Other Paths to Parenthood
Chapter 9 171
When Things Go Right: Pregnancy After Infertility
Afterword 187
The Journey Never Truly Ends
Appendix A 193
Recommended Media (as of 2022)
Appendix B 195
Terms and Acronyms
Acknowledgments 199

WELCOME NOTE

FROM THE IVF DAD

If you're reading this, I assume you're where I was several years ago—having tried to make a baby without success. I'm sorry. There's no elegant way to put it: infertility sucks.

I'll tell you all about me and my wife's difficult experience in the pages ahead. One thing that kept me going throughout is my resolve to connect with other people who are experiencing the same thing. Infertility can be lonely, and society discourages people—men in particular—from talking about our struggles. I want to help change that, at least for those of us going through infertility. My dream is to build a community of men experiencing infertility who feel knowledgeable and well-equipped to tread the path ahead with strength and a burly, strapping, manly dose of sensitivity. And for the women who are also reading this, my hope is that this book provides a jumping off point to help your partner be engaged and supportive.

I hope this book helps you understand the path ahead and options for treatment. Moreover, I hope it helps you make sense of how you and your partner are feeling during this difficult time, and gives you plenty of simple ideas and strategies to get through it. You might even come out on the other side stronger than you are now.

Please keep in touch—seriously. You can connect with me on Instagram @TheIVFDad, on TheIVFDad.com, or via email at TheIVFDad@gmail.com. Reach out! I'd love to hear from you.

Now let's get started.

—Keegan, The IVF Dad

INTRODUCTION

A swarm of spidermen, ninjas, and princesses scurried up and down the block. Dusk settled in, golden hues giving way to deep blue as jack-o-lanterns lit the way toward the night's candy haul. And on our porch, in our white house with green shutters on the end of the street, my wife Olivia and I awaited the onslaught, hundreds of pieces of candy at the ready.

In our small Victorian village in upstate New York, Halloween is a big deal. Hundreds of kids criss-cross the streets seeking to load their baskets and bags with treats. Families travel into the village and park from miles away, knowing the tree-lined streets are safe and easy to traverse, while kids relish the sheer volume of houses they can attack one by one.

It's a special time for the whole town; a festive night in which the best characteristics of the close-knit village community are on display. But this Halloween night was a uniquely special one for me and Olivia.

Earlier that afternoon, we received news we had anticipated for a very long time. We had completed our first IVF embryo transfer about two weeks prior. Earlier that morning, Olivia had left just as the sun rose to have her blood drawn and find out if the transfer had worked and resulted in a pregnancy. Our fertility clinic nurse Jennifer—who supported us through the entire process, and is a candidate for sainthood in our book—called around noon and left a voicemail with the results. We left work early and came home so we could listen to the voicemail together. Hearts pounding, we pressed play.

Jennifer was upbeat, getting right to the punchline: "Congratulations: you're pregnant! We'll do another blood check in two days."

It had been a long road; nearly two years had passed since we first started trying to start a family. Olivia and I embraced, feeling thrilled and overwhelmed and relieved. The news that we would be parents made an already exciting day even sweeter. We lined up spooky orange luminarias to light the path to our porch and filled candy bowls to the brim.

As the rush of costumed children slowed to a trickle, I placed my hand on her stomach. I knew the embryo was still microscopic and a baby bump was months away, but after such a long wait I couldn't resist. We talked of potential baby costumes and critiqued each one as they walked away; a little boy dressed as Bob Ross carrying an enormous palette dappled with happy greens was undoubtedly the best of the night.

"Next year, we'll have our own little one to dress up," I beamed.

~ ~ ~

Five weeks later, I looked out on another fading sunset. This early winter dusk was far removed from that golden October evening. The dank gray sky seemed stained; the sun slouched across the horizon.

I was in a small patient room in the labor and delivery ward of our local hospital. Olivia was just down the hall, under anesthesia, having the remains of the embryo we had celebrated on Halloween removed from her via an operation called a dilation and curettage, or D&C.

Our initial excitement from Halloween didn't last long. At the next blood draw check-in, we learned the level of the pregnancy hormone human chorionic gonadotropin, or hCG, in Olivia's blood was not rising as quickly as it should. The clinic continued to check the level. One day the hCG would shoot up and offer a glimmer of hope; a few days later it would stagnate, accompanied by Jennifer's sobering words of wisdom: "Keep your fingers crossed, but it doesn't look good."

After a few weeks of this limbo, we reached the point where an ultrasound was possible to get more clarity. The initial results were inconclusive. The embryo showed some growth, but after another couple weeks of waiting and checking, there wasn't enough development. Two days before Thanksgiving, we got the final diagnosis: the pregnancy resulted in a blighted ovum—basically an empty embryo that doesn't develop. Put more simply: it was a miscarriage.

The clinic told Olivia to stop taking all shots and drugs (another twist in the road of IVF: the shots, pills, and blood draws don't necessarily end once you're pregnant). They laid out our options: wait for the miscarriage to start on its own, take a pill that would force her body to start the miscarriage process, or try to get into the hospital for a D&C.

There was no availability at the hospital, so we opted for the pill. Like everything else in the prior six weeks, it didn't go to plan. Olivia took the pill. She endured excruciating cramps while we sat on our couch debating whether we could attend Thanksgiving. We later learned the pill forces your body to have labor contractions, thus expelling (usually) the contents of the uterus. But nothing came out.

Meanwhile, I spent these weeks cycling between disbelief, deep sadness, and attempts to stay strong and be supportive for Olivia. I felt dazed and disinterested completing everyday tasks like commuting, attending work meetings, and folding laundry. I couldn't bear the sight of babies or kids, something that usually gave me a lot of joy. With such an awful thing happening to us, it seemed that the world should grind to a halt in recognition of our pain. But of course it didn't.

And so, at last, unable to succeed at even having a miscarriage that goes normally, we ended up in the hospital on a bleak early December evening. As a final cruelty, we discovered the D&C procedure is performed in the labor and delivery ward. Walking in, we passed the family waiting area where eager fathers- and grandparents-to-be awaited the news of their baby's arrival. We commiserated with the kind middle-aged check-in lady who agreed it was a special kind of torture to make us come to labor and delivery for the awful operation that was about to take place.

Three hours later, we left the hospital and drove home to our white and green-shuttered house in our little Victorian village. Defeated, and back at square one, I thought back on my premature Halloween night celebration. All I could do was shake my head at how foolish it seemed now.

~ ~ ~

Welcome to the Infertility Yo-Yo

If you're reading this book, you're probably already familiar with what I call the *infertility yo-yo*—the endless ups and downs you experience when unfortunate enough to be taking the "long road" to parenthood.

If you're reading this book, you probably started out much like we did at some point, perhaps six months ago, or perhaps two or three or even five years ago: you decide it's time to start trying for a family, you "pull the goalie," and at first, it's exciting! We're trying to have a kid (you think)! We'll probably be pregnant within a few months (you think)! Maybe you talk about possible kid names, start looking at the endless reel of silly gender reveal videos on the internet, and plot ways to surprise the family with the news in a few months (YOU THINK!).

If you're reading this book, you also probably know how it feels when, after several months of trying, the early excitement starts to wane. As each month's cycle comes and goes, the initial reaction of "*hey, no one gets it right off the bat, it'll happen soon enough*" slowly morphs into a less assured "*well...maybe next month will be our time.*"

And if you're reading this book, you probably know that's when the real descent begins. Then the crazy thoughts creep in. *Maybe we need to make sure we do it in this position.* Or, *I read something that said that you should put your legs above your head for at least ten and a half minutes after sex.* Or, *what if that thing I ate/that scented laundry detergent we use/that intense exercise class I did/the time Greg Paulson threw a football at my groin in sixth grade...might be causing a problem?* Which of course all leads to the ultimate question you (and your partner) have probably already thought about: *What if something's really wrong here?*

If you're reading this book, you may already be delving into the vast and initially confusing world of potential causes of infertility, treatments for infertility, statistics about likelihood of success, and of course everyone's favorite topic: the cost of treatments! And then there are the acronyms. Between IVF, IUI, ICSI, PGT, PGS, and hCG, your brain may already be spinning. Don't worry—I'll demystify all of this later.

But before we go on, if you're reading this book, there are two critical things you should know. These two things may help more than anything else as you move ahead.

First: **You and your partner are not alone.** In fact, according to RESOLVE, the National Infertility Association, approximately *one out of every eight* couples in the United States experiences infertility. Struggling to have a baby can feel lonely and isolating, and with good reason. Couples experiencing infertility are often at a point in life where every other couple they know is also trying to have children, and it will feel like every single other couple is having wild and instantaneous success in the endeavor. "We're expecting!" announcements will crop up like an invasive species in your text messages and news feed, just as the wedding invitations arrived in your mailbox in a regular cadence a few years prior. But that statistic bears repeating: *one in eight couples will experience infertility.*

So remember, you are not walking this path by yourself. Just by starting this book, learning more about your options, discussing this information with your partner, and reaching out to other people who are currently or have been in your shoes, you're taking huge steps toward progress.

The second thing to know: if you only do one thing today to help make your journey easier, **reach out to others and talk about what you're going through**. The old adage that "a problem shared is a problem halved" couldn't be more true. I guarantee you'll find a sympathetic ear at the minimum, and more likely you'll find there are far more people you know who are among the one in eight than you thought.

Unfortunately none of us has a crystal ball to determine exactly when or how our infertility comes to a resolution and we get to banish the *yo-yo* forever, but my hope is this book makes the path there a bit smoother.

WHY DID I WRITE THIS BOOK, AND WHY SHOULD YOU BOTHER TO READ IT?

The short answer? Because infertility sucks, and especially sucks if you feel alone when you're going through it.

But for a slightly longer answer: Most of the resources and books on infertility are centered on a woman's experience, and understandably so. Women generally bear the brunt of surgeries, pokes, prods, blood work, surges of natural and artificial hormones, and other pains and difficulties of fertility treatments.

However, resources designed to support men experiencing infertility were much harder to find. I listened to countless podcasts, browsed social media accounts, and read dozens (if not hundreds) of blogs and articles about fertility treatments, most of which were hosted and written by women (again, understandably). And to be clear, those podcasts and other resources were incredibly helpful!

On a rare occasion I'd come across a conversation in which both partners from a couple were interviewed, and it was great to hear both perspectives.[1] But those examples were rare. And unfortunately, when I did find resources geared toward men, they generally spoke to and about men as if we're all underdeveloped neanderthals. Everything had to be couched in goofy humor, football references, or comparisons to beer and chicken wings. I love beer and chicken wings, but I wanted a resource that talks to men like we're actually smart.

Here's what I learned in discussions with other men who experienced infertility: *men just want to be empowered, supportive partners.* But men often feel overwhelmed, confused, and poorly equipped to navigate such a difficult experience as infertility.

So I wanted to fix that. Every time I've talked with another dad who experienced infertility, I felt barriers break down. Infertility is something that other people can sympathize with, but unless they've been through it, they'll never quite *get it.* They can't understand why you suddenly aren't excited to talk about kids like you used to be. They don't get what it's like to wonder if you're ever going to be able to play catch or read books with your children. They don't understand how it feels when, instead of getting pregnant the old fashioned way, you have to set an alarm every night to remind you when it's time to fill up a syringe with hormones and give your wife a shot.

---

[1] A notable and great example of this is the podcast IVFML, which features husband and wife team Simon Ganz and Anna Almendrala. I can't recommend it highly enough. It's honest, hilarious, and informative. Go download it, and see Appendix A for more recommended podcasts and media.

So simply put—this book is for you. If you're a man who wants to better understand how infertility treatment works, this book is for you. If you're a woman who wants to give their partner a great tool to become more informed and supportive along your infertility journey, this book is for you. If you're a couple who's just trying to muddle through the awful infertility muck, it's definitely for you—both of you!

I'll consider this book a success if even one guy or couple out there picks it up, reads it, and feels a little less lonely. And feel free to skip around if it helps. You can jump in anywhere, and come back to other chapters later. Hopefully along the way, you'll feel more confident about navigating this crazy yo-yo, and better equipped to support yourself and your partner.

Manhood, Fatherhood, and Messages

My advice above to reach out and share what you're going through might have made you think: "Hold on, I'm not ready to go sharing my business with people." That's a very normal thing to feel. I know this isn't easy, because there are a lot of factors that make it harder for men to talk about things they're struggling with.

Here's a quick list of some of the most common messages we hear as men from media and society. As you read through them, consider the following: Do these sound familiar?; Where might these ideas come from?; and, How much does this idea affect me and my life? If you believe them strongly, don't feel bad or as if you've done something "wrong"—there's no point in getting down on ourselves, and remember, absorbing these messages is normal because we hear them constantly:

- Men address problems by taking action; guys fix things.
- Man up!

- Men shouldn't show too much emotion, it makes them look weak.
- Boys don't cry.
- Men shouldn't ask for help. Real men help themselves.
- Men shouldn't talk about their feelings, especially more challenging things like feeling sad or anxious, and especially shouldn't share them with other men.
- True men are strong and silent.
- A real guy can "get his wife pregnant" without any trouble.
- Fathers provide material goods and money for the family.
- Be a man.
- Real guys don't wear X type of clothes/listen to Y type of music, (or fill in the blank with hundreds of other examples!)
- Being a father is part of what makes somebody a man.

Unless you've been living under a rock, these ideas probably sound familiar. In fact, you might really resonate with these ideas! After all, think about one of the most popular and revered male characters of all time, James Bond—he's constantly taking action, physically strong, and almost never shows emotion. While the media has made some strides in recent years in painting a more complete and diverse representation of everyone, including men who don't fit these stereotypical molds, these ideas still run deep within most of us. Experiencing infertility showed me I had really absorbed a lot of these ideas. Changing my thinking wasn't simple, but it was critical to keeping perspective on things during our journey.

I'm sharing this up front because I think it's a particular challenge for men going through infertility. As I mentioned above, I struggled with a few of the ideas above throughout our journey. I definitely resonated with the idea that men face problems by trying to take action and fix them. For me, this showed up as a habit of obsessively Googling to try to learn everything possible about infertility, different treatments, and how any small part of my or Olivia's health history might hold a clue to something we could do to "fix" things and get pregnant. I also spent time dealing with the ideas that men shouldn't ask for help or show their feelings. I was hesitant to tell anyone what we were going through, worrying (however irrationally) that people would think this struggle or my sadness about it were something to be pitied, or a sign of weakness.

One of the more challenging of these ideas for many men is the last one on the list, that being a "real man" and being a "father" are deeply connected. While fatherhood is indeed one experience a man may have, this becomes a problem when we connect being a man and being a father too closely. Particularly if we find out there are issues with our sperm, this can lead us to think we're not "manly" and perhaps not cut out to be a father.

These are real and difficult feelings—and ones we can work to challenge. But these ideas don't just go away overnight—I still work to this day to challenge these ideas whenever they crop up in my mind. I'll return to this often throughout the book with suggestions for how to start understanding these messages and our reactions to them. It isn't easy, but remember that it is natural to absorb these messages, and also totally possible to change our thinking.

To start, consider a few of these alternative ideas to those above—they may not sound very natural now, but try them out for size. Write them down or say them out loud to yourself ten times every day for a week. See if you notice even a gradual change.

- Strong people aren't afraid to reach out for help when they need it.
- Sharing problems can be a great way to get support.
- Talking about how I'm feeling allows me to be a better partner.

- Getting more comfortable with discussing things I'm struggling with will prepare me to be a better father, because I know that's a tough job!
- I can prepare myself to be a great father.
- I get to define what it means to me to be a great father.

BRIEF NOTES ON WORD-CHOICE AND PERSPECTIVE

With this stage setting complete, it's about time to start. There are just a couple quick notes and caveats I should share:

First, I use the terms "you" and "your partner" throughout the book. By "you," I mean the person with a penis and sperm, which I'm referring to as the "man". By "your partner," I mean the person with a vagina and uterus, which I'm referring to as the "woman". I understand and respect that people and relationships come in many forms, so I've chosen this wording for simplicity of writing only, and not as any reflection of my personal beliefs on gender or partnership.

Second, this book is based on my perspective, my experience, and the many things I've learned and researched over five years of infertility. It's meant to help you understand what the journey might look like, and how to support yourself and your partner along the way. *I strive to ensure every word in here provides accurate information as of the date of publishing. However, this book is for educational purposes and is in no way intended to substitute for the advice of a licensed medical professional. Always consult with a properly licensed medical professional in any matters related to your health and your partner's health.*

Finally, my perspective is limited and doesn't capture all the different experiences humans have relating to infertility and the quest for parenthood.

I'm a man whose partner is a woman, and we are fortunate to have good health insurance coverage. Writing from this perspective in no way intends to exclude or diminish others who are going through the journey to build a family, whether they're same-sex couples, hopeful single parents, couples and partners with limited financial resources, or any of a million other permutations. There are lots of great blogs, social media profiles, books, podcasts, and other resources which capture a variety of perspectives well, many of which are listed in Appendix A. Check them out, and if you're overwhelmed by the options, I'd recommend starting with the podcast Infertile AF. It's a wonderful, informative, real, honest, funny, and relatable show which gives a great overview of the world of infertility through stories of people who've been through it.

With those notes explained, it's time to dive in—and we'll start, of course, at the beginning.

CHAPTER 1

STEP ONE IS ACCEPTING: WHEN "TRYING" ISN'T "WORKING"

"Ugh. My period's here," Olivia called down the hall. I didn't need to see her to visualize her crestfallen face.

I had been puttering in the bedroom, but now my shoulders slumped. I sighed and lay down on the bed. It was the middle of January, and the brown-gray landscape and frigid cold of upstate New York mirrored our mood.

By this time, about six months after we'd started trying to conceive, these were the last words Olivia hoped to say each month and the last ones I hoped to hear. But they stung a bit harder this time. This time, Olivia's period was several days late. Naturally, as the few days passed beyond when we expected it to arrive, our excitement grew. We started to plan: how much longer until we're confident enough to take a pregnancy test? Tomorrow? The day after?

The prospect of finally being able to take a pregnancy test was exciting and nerve-wracking all at once. We even had a box of two tests in a bathroom drawer, purchased in the halcyon days when we were certain a pregnancy would come easily and quickly.

We had just started to feel that glimmer of hope: maybe...just maybe...our time had finally come. But it wasn't to be. The pregnancy test remained shoved deep in the back of a bathroom drawer, just as it had been for months.

Late in the afternoon we went out to walk in the setting midwinter sun. We're walkers and always have been—it provides special time for Olivia and me. We walk and talk. We connect. We planned our wedding on long walks. We mused about what it would be like to have kids on long walks. On our long walks in Brooklyn, before we moved upstate, we dreamed about the house and the lawn and the dog we would get.

On our long walk that day in January, we shared our worries about not yet being pregnant. We had always known we wanted to have kids, but at that point we both had a nagging feeling that the old-fashioned way...might not work for us.

~ ~ ~

HOW DO YOU KNOW WHEN TRYING ISN'T WORKING?

After our chilly stroll, we decided to start doing some research. It had been just over six months since we started trying to get pregnant. Most of the resources we found told us the same simple rule of thumb: If the woman is under 35, you should seek medical advice if you're not pregnant within a year. If the woman is 35 or older, seek medical advice if not pregnant within six months. Olivia was under 35, but we decided not to wait the additional six months. She made an appointment with her OB/GYN for a check-up to discuss our concerns.

This illustrates the frustrating reality of infertility—general expectations and rules of thumb are just that: general. Every individual case is different, and there are many potential causes for infertility as well as exceptions to every rule.

For instance, here are some situations which might lead to you seek medical advice earlier than the rule of thumb above—or maybe before you even start trying to conceive:

- You and/or your partner are over 35 (and especially if over 40)
- You or your partner have had prior surgery involving your reproductive apparatus
- You or your partner have pre-existing health issues involving your reproductive apparatus, such as testicular cancer for you (which is most common in younger men), or endometriosis for your partner (a common condition which causes extremely painful and/or irregular periods)
- You or your partner have a history of infertility in close family members (parents, grandparents, siblings)
- You have had a prior semen analysis that revealed low sperm count or sperm abnormalities
- Your partner has irregular or infrequent periods

These are just a few examples, but you get the gist: if you or your partner have any sort of condition or issue that could affect your reproduction, it may be better to get checked out proactively before you start to try to get pregnant, or closer to the "six months" end of the rule of thumb from above.

In our case, we trusted our instincts and decided it was better to get checked out on the early side. We knew it was possible it might just take a few more months, but we also wanted to be proactive. We hadn't reached the one year mark of trying, but our dream was to have two or three kids. And of course, our research had also pointed us into the world of infertility stories; we quickly learned that infertility treatment can take years to work (if it ever works at all). With both of us approaching our mid-30s, we figured it was better to check everything out earlier.

The takeaway? Use the rules of thumb and information above to help figure out if trying isn't working, but ultimately trust your gut. You and your partner know what your hopes are for your family, so don't hesitate to be proactive and seek out professional medical advice.

Are You Trying at the Right Time? (What They Didn't Teach You in High School Health...)

All the above said, there is one critical thing we learned through our research that seems obvious in retrospect, but can totally derail your chances to get pregnant: *there is an optimal time during a woman's cycle when having sex is most likely to result in pregnancy—and likewise, there are times during the cycle when having sex is least likely to result in pregnancy.* In other words, *when* you have sex matters! I know this may come as a shock. In middle and high school health class, we were all led to believe that splitting an ice cream cone or dancing too closely with a woman might cause pregnancy if you weren't careful.

But jokes aside, timing really can make the difference. We have friends (with a beautiful baby) who are living proof. They tried to conceive for months without success, then discovered that when they had sex actually mattered. Shortly thereafter, they were expecting.

So what is this magical formula? The general rule of thumb is: *a woman's most fertile window is when she ovulates, which is roughly 14 days before her period starts.* Having sex around that time gives you the best chance of conceiving. Now this isn't to say you can't get pregnant by having sex at other times in the cycle—it's just less probable.

And why is this the case? Well, a lot has to line up for conception to happen. The egg is released (or ovulated) about 14 days before a woman's period starts, about half way through a typical 28 day menstrual cycle. Sperm have to be present around that time, and must make their way on the long and perilous journey through the cervix (the opening at the top of the vagina) into the uterus and on to the fallopian tubes, where they must find and fertilize an egg.

The cervix also acts as a gatekeeper: it's softer and more open around ovulation to make it easier for sperm to enter. At other times during the cycle, the cervix is harder and more closed off, hence, more difficult for sperm to enter.

All of these factors make it far easier for sperm and egg to meet if you time sex around the magical ovulation period, give or take 2-3 days (there's some flexibility due to another fun fact—sperm can survive in the uterus and fallopian tubes for 1-5 days).

Now there's one more complication here: this relies on having a fairly regular period, which many women do not. Some women's cycles are not entirely predictable or only come every few months. Some women may have periods but not actually ovulate. If this is the case with your partner, all the more reason to seek medical advice. In some cases, doctors may prescribe medications to help regulate or induce ovulation.

That all said, how do you make sure you're trying at the right time? There are a few tools to help you, and books and resources that explain the methods, such as *Taking Charge of Your Fertility* by Toni Wechsler (see Appendix A for books and other media recommendations).

- The easiest way to tell if your partner is ovulating is for her to use Ovulation Test Strips (sometimes called LH Test Strips after "luteinizing hormone," the hormone that shows when ovulation is imminent.) Your partner dunks the test strip in her urine (follow directions on the box) and the test strip tells if LH is present. If it is, that means it's time to get busy.
- Another more labor intensive (for your partner) way to track ovulation is by taking her basal body temperature. Essentially,

> she needs to take her temperature vaginally first thing upon waking every morning and to track the temperature. The temperature remains steady, then jumps up about a degree upon ovulation and remains higher until just before her next period begins. The best time to have sex for conception is the couple days prior to the jump in temperature. By charting her basal body temperature, you can get a better idea about when ovulation generally happens during her cycles. This can be particularly helpful if they don't fit the usual "28 day" mold.

If you aren't sure if you've been trying at the right time, these simple fixes could work for you. If they do, then pop a bottle of champagne for you and sparkling cider for your partner, because you've figured it out! If not, you're still in good company.

Maintaining Healthy Swimmers

Before we dive into what to do if you've decided trying isn't working, it's important to take stock of your own physical health and consider any steps that could help you produce strong and healthy sperm. So much about infertility is out of our control, but this is one area where our lifestyle may slightly improve our chances of success.

A quick sidebar: I'm using the terms "sperm" and "semen." To ensure the difference is clear, "sperm" refers to the individual gamete cells with the little oval-ish heads and long tails which can penetrate and fertilize an egg. "Semen" refers to the substance that comes out when men ejaculate, which includes both sperm and the many other components and nutrients within the jelly-like liquid.

Making this more complicated, it's easy to believe that our "manhood" or "manliness" correlates with our sperm count—if we find out we have 25 million sperm in each ejaculation and the guy down the street has 350 million, our first thought would probably be something like "Well, I guess I'm a real wimp."

As I wrote in the first chapter, we need to work to decouple some of the ideas society puts in our head about what being a "man" or "manly" means. Your capacity to produce a certain number of sperm says nothing about how "manly" you are, nor how good a father you will be. To help make this shift, you may want to think about what you'd like your future children to say about you when they're older. My guess is your list of things would include items along the lines of "he always believes in me" and "he always takes time to show me he cares," and not "he had the highest sperm count of any man in Sheboygan!" It sounds silly, but going through infertility will bring up issues for us around what we believe and what society has told us about masculinity—challenging those ideas will help make the journey easier and help you ultimately become a better parent.

All this said, let's look at how lifestyle changes might lead to slight improvements in sperm quality. To do that, we first need to know how sperm are made. Our testes normally produce millions of sperm every several hours. After their "birth" in the testicles, those millions of little swimmers head into a tube called the epididymis. There, they spend about five weeks growing and developing, eventually making it into another tube called the vas deferens. At the point where they (and you) are lucky enough to achieve ejaculation, the sperm mix with seminal fluid and spurt from the vas deferens and out through the urethra. This usually totals about 2-5 milliliters of semen, containing an average of 100 million sperm per milliliter.

This is grossly oversimplified, but you can see how much goes into the development of each tiny sperm. It also explains why it's important to dedicate time heading into potential fertility treatment to make healthy lifestyle choices. It takes time to make sperm, and guidance from the

American Society for Reproductive Medicine suggests it takes a minimum of three months of lifestyle changes to improve sperm quality.

A critical disclaimer here: there are also genetic and physical variations from person to person which can cause men to have different sperm counts and percentages of "normal" sperm. There are also environmental factors men in more recent generations have been exposed to that our grandfathers and ancestors never experienced—things like low-level radiation from laptops (see below), plastics, artificial fragrances, and other new materials. This isn't to say any of these things are inherently bad, it's merely to point out that much about our sperm health is out of our control.

So what kind of lifestyle choices might help? Here are a few tips to get you started, which probably won't be terribly surprising:

- *Exercise regularly.* This can boost testosterone levels and improve the quality of your semen. I'm not a natural exerciser, but walking the dog or going to the gym where I can watch some TV for an hour on a bike or treadmill, plus an occasional yoga class, works for me. You'll figure out what works for you.
- *Take steps to de-stress.* There are many suggestions in the chapters that follow on strategies to do this, but consider doing short guided meditations from an app or a website, taking five minutes to do deep breathing, or just going for a walk in nature for a bit each day if you can.
- *Stop smoking.* Enough said here, but smoking is unhealthy for all sorts of reasons, and can negatively impact your semen and sperm quality.
- *Limit alcohol intake.* There's no need to become a teetotaler (a nightly glass of red wine was a necessary relaxant for me during our infertility and beyond), but if you're regularly having more

than a drink or two per day, it can have detrimental effects on your testosterone and semen quality.

- *Keep phones/tablets/computers off your junk.* The combination of heat and radiation could potentially hurt swimmers. Keep your phone in your back pocket and computer/laptop on a desk instead of in your lap when possible.
- *Talk to your doctor about any possible dietary changes or supplements that could help.* There are a million and one articles on the internet claiming that this vitamin, that supplement, or this food can help boost men's fertility. Check them out, but always ask and follow your doctor's advice.

You can find plenty of other advice out there on lifestyle choices to give yourself the best chance for conception. Your partner may also be looking to lifestyle choices to support her fertility. Be a team player—while some things you're working on may not necessarily apply to your partner and vice versa, talk through the list above and any other recommendations your doctors have made. Could you start going to the gym together? Start cooking a couple more meals at home each week with healthier ingredients? Pick a few things and work on them together. It'll strengthen your teamwork and help you both feel your best for any potential treatments.

Also remember your partner may be particularly affected by suggestions about exercise and diet. Just as men receive really awful messages from society and the media about stifling our emotions and not asking for help, women are bombarded with toxic messages about what they should eat and how their bodies should look. Bear this in mind and ask her about this. It could lead to a great conversation, and open up a chance for you to talk through the messages we receive as men.

~ ~ ~

As we walked around the village that dark afternoon, feeling sullen, we initially trudged along in silence. Over time though, we started discussing lots of questions. I'm more reserved, but Olivia is always good at starting a conversation. I often jokingly call her "Barbara Walters," as her ability to get anyone to talk about anything is both impressive and mysterious to me, as I'm more comfortable getting a root canal than making small talk with most people.

She turned to me about halfway down our street: "So what do you think about this whole thing—where we are with trying to become parents, all of it?"

"Well..." I pondered a moment. "I guess I mainly feel frustrated. When we started trying, I remember talking about having a baby in a year. Now here we are, almost a year later. I feel stupid for assuming it would be easy." I had learned by observing Olivia's conversational skill to turn the question back. "How do you feel about it?"

"The same. And just...sad." Her voice started to break. She breathed deeply, then went on. "Just really sad. We were so excited to become parents. I'm still excited. We have this beautiful house, we have friends who are having kids. I just had this picture in my mind of us, playing with the kids in the backyard...and now..."

After a moment, I jumped in. "I know, it feels like...will that ever happen? It's scary to think about that. It's not how I pictured our life. I mean, it's not how we pictured it."

We shuffled ahead for another minute or two in silence.

"So what do we do?" asked Olivia.

"I don't know," I said. "I know there are treatments like IVF but I'm not even sure where you go for that type of thing. I don't even know if we need it. I guess we need to start looking at some of that stuff and trying to learn. But is that just giving up? I mean...we can keep trying. Who knows? Maybe next month it'll work."

"It hasn't worked for almost a year," Olivia sputtered acridly.

"Alright, alright." I could tell Olivia was upset, so I took a moment to come back to reality. "You're right. So, what if we both start to do a little research? Then, if in a few days we still feel like we need to, you could schedule an appointment with your OB. I mean, I don't know what they'll do, but we can at least start getting things checked out. And who knows, it might take months to get in for an appointment."

"Ok," Olivia replied, sniffling slightly. "I just never ever imagined this could happen. Never."

~ ~ ~

ALRIGHT, WE'RE WONDERING IF TRYING MAY NOT BE WORKING AND WANT TO TAKE STEPS. WHAT DO WE DO NEXT?

I know this isn't an easy step to take. As our conversation on that cold day showed, admitting that something may not be working can be very hard. However, in this day and age, we're fortunate that help and treatment is better understood, more advanced, and more available than ever before.

Before we get to the actual steps of testing for a diagnosis and talking about potential treatments with a doctor, I'd recommend you do a couple of things during this time to prepare yourself and help you feel more comfortable navigating possible conversations to come. (Note you can do this at the same time as you start scheduling medical tests—as we all know, the time from calling to get an appointment to actually getting in for any tests to getting those results back and discussing them with a doctor can take several weeks—or months. So kill two birds with one stone and start doing these first few steps at the same time as you start making appointments.)

First, make time to check in with your partner and discuss how you're both feeling.

Just like Olivia and I did on that walk around the village, it's important to take time for a frank conversation about how you're both feeling. At this early stage, it might be easiest to start with the question she asked me: "*How are you feeling about where we're at with our journey toward parenthood?*"

The conversation might be difficult, but the importance of communicating openly with your partner will set a strong foundation to carry you through your journey to parenthood, no matter what challenges you encounter along the way.

Second, take some time to learn about fertility treatments: listen to podcasts, read books and articles, and so forth (see Appendix A for a full list of recommended media).

If you've looked at all into infertility treatment, you've undoubtedly realized there's an entire dictionary of terms and acronyms (Appendix B!). At first this will be overwhelming. Early in our journey, I devoured infertility podcasts on my way to and from work. While I initially didn't know an IVF from an ICSI, I eventually learned. Having this general knowledge provided at least some small bit of control. It really helped to start getting familiar with these things early on in the process.

Remember: the point of this research is to empower you. It's to provide an opportunity to get more comfortable with the terminology, so you can be a better advocate for yourself and your partner when you actually start going into conversations about diagnoses and potential treatments. If you're comfortable at this point, I'd also recommend looking at the options and process around adoption, surrogacy, fostering, and other paths to parenthood (more on this in chapter 9). There are entire books dedicated to these topics, but it can be useful to start some research early to understand the landscape, as well as what you and your partner feel about other potential paths to build your family.

This research will also come in handy if and when you and your partner find yourselves discussing options with your medical team. You may be blessed with doctors and nurses who are able to explain medical terms in a clear and straightforward manner, but we all know that's not always the case. In addition, time is often short in medical appointments. Having a good basic understanding of the terms and potential treatments ensures you're empowered to actively participate in the conversation and ask the right questions.

To illustrate the importance, compare these two conversations showing what your first meeting with the fertility doctor might sound like:

- Conversation A
    - DOCTOR: Based on your tests, you have low AMH and possible DOR. In addition, your semen analysis revealed low motility. I recommend we start IVF with ICSI and PGD as soon as possible.
    - YOU: *Sweating, embarrassed you don't understand, trying to guess W-T-F I-C-S-I even means*
    - YOUR PARTNER: *Looking nervously to see what you think, then in a small voice:* I um…think that sounds ok to us, Doctor?
- Conversation B
    - DOCTOR: Based on your tests, you have low AMH and possible DOR. In addition, your semen analysis revealed low motility. I recommend we start IVF with ICSI and PGD as soon as possible.

- YOU: Got it, let me make sure I understand. So you're saying there may be some egg quality issues and that there are issues with my sperm as well?
- YOUR PARTNER: And that using IVF is our best option. What do you see as our chances of success if we follow that course?

See the difference? You don't have to memorize a reproductive endocrinology textbook, but you'll be better equipped to handle complex medical information in a situation where you may not have much time with your doctor, and you may be under some pressure to understand the options presented. You'll also eventually start to understand common scenarios so that if you, for instance, find out you have a low sperm count, you may have already listened to some podcasts that discuss treatment options and perhaps even share some stories of a couple who found success with the same diagnosis.

I know this isn't easy, but the great news is you're reading this book, which means you're already taking charge! I truly hope reading it helps you feel more in control of the process, the possible treatments, and your options at every step of the way. And with how much often feels out of our control when going through fertility treatment, this knowledge can be so powerful.

Third, start researching your options for doctors and fertility clinics should you and your partner end up seeking treatment.

The point of this initial research is just to get you comfortable and to understand what options are out there for you and your partner. You may have several fertility clinics within driving distance, or the closest clinic may be hundreds of miles away. Some clinics may be smaller and more individualized, while others may be capable of managing very large caseloads. There are even a growing number of clinics specializing in providing lower-cost out of pocket treatment by serving a high volume of clients from around the country and world, many of whom fly to where the clinic is located for certain parts of the treatment.

There are pros and cons to every clinic, and some research will help you determine what is right for you. You may be really interested in personalized service and opt for a smaller clinic, but end up paying more. You may be most interested in the price and opt to fly out to a clinic that offers lower pricing, knowing that the customer service and care might not be quite as individualized.

Don't be afraid to schedule introductory meetings with several clinics to get multiple opinions after your baseline testing is complete. You may get an opportunity to meet some of the doctors and staff who would be treating you. Many clinics also have videos and other media on their websites to help you get to know their approach, and some even offer live video call introduction sessions either individually or to groups.

In the end, you and your partner will probably choose a doctor based on a combination of what makes sense financially, what makes sense in terms of location, the advice and reviews of others, and of course your gut feeling about the office and doctors. Finding a clinic and medical team you are comfortable with can significantly ease the stress of treatments, so this time is well worth the effort. We'll delve into this in much greater depth in chapter 4 as well, which is all about finding the right clinic for you.

Fourth, start looking at the costs of treatment, your health insurance (if you have coverage), and think through possible plans depending on what type of treatment you may require.

One of the cruel realities of infertility treatments is that they are (in general) extremely expensive. I hope you're among the fortunate folks out there with good medical insurance coverage including at least some benefits for fertility treatments. But many people do not have insurance coverage for fertility treatments, so it's an excellent idea to start wrapping your head around how to afford treatment, and to at least think through potential plans based on a range of possible treatment options. There's no easy answer here, but at least knowing what you may face can help make it seem a bit less daunting.

Here are some general tips to get started. First, for those without insurance coverage, look again at those fertility clinics you researched in the third step. In general, most private fertility clinics in the US will post some numbers detailing costs of services. Just be aware the "sticker" cost may not include everything required for a treatment cycle; for instance, a clinic may advertise "IUI for $995" but not mention that you may need to purchase a variety of drugs that could add hundreds or thousands of dollars to the total cost.

Even for those lucky enough to have fertility treatments covered by your health insurance, be sure to do your due diligence and look at the fine print. I'd strongly recommend calling your insurance company to discuss the benefits and ensure you fully understand WHAT is covered, and if there are any conditions to qualify for the coverage.

We were among the fortunate people who had great health coverage for fertility treatment, but one thing we found out very early is that our first insurance carrier would not approve benefits for IVF treatment until we had tried three "rounds" of a lower level intervention. We later switched insurance between two rounds of IVF and found out that the previous insurance had covered procedures (i.e. egg retrieval surgery, etc.) as well as prescriptions, while the new insurance covered procedures only and not prescriptions. This was a major change, as the prescriptions for IVF can often cost hundreds or even thousands of dollars. As if these two changes weren't enough, we received notice two months before a subsequent planned IVF round that our clinic would no longer accept our insurance plan. Fortunately, we were in open enrollment and had other plans available with coverage our clinic accepted. These three small anecdotes should illustrate the need to do your homework and spend some time learning about managing insurance, if you have coverage. If you end up pursuing treatment, the fertility clinic should also have finance staff to help you navigate the process.

I'd also recommend looking at costs of other possible paths to parenthood such as adoption, surrogacy, and fostering. While you may not end up using any of these paths, we found it helpful to understand basic information about how they work and what they cost. For instance, we were surprised to learn the average cost of an adoption from start to finish is anywhere from $15,000-$40,000 or more according to the Child Welfare Information Gateway.

Now that you've started to have some in-depth talks with your partner, and done some work to understand the terms, treatment options, and expenses associated with infertility treatments, let's first take a quick breath. If you're feeling overwhelmed, this is normal. If you're feeling anxious, this is normal. This is a very complicated process, but trust me: you will get more comfortable with the terms over time, and with dedication, will find a path to parenthood that works for you.

OK, I TOOK A DEEP BREATH AND MY HEART RATE HAS RETURNED TO A SEMI-NORMAL STATE. HOW DO WE GET STARTED PURSUING MEDICAL HELP?

Excellent—take one more deep breath. Repeat after me: It's OK to feel overwhelmed by all this. Now, here are the actual medical steps you'll need to take to move toward testing and understanding what may be going on.

The first step is making appropriate medical appointments to get you and your partner's reproductive apparatus checked out.

As with pretty much all fertility treatment, you get the easy part here: a semen analysis. This is basically what you'd picture: you ejaculate in a cup, hand it over to a lab, and they do a deep dive on your swimmers. The lab will analyze how many sperm you produce in each "load," and the percent of those sperm that are "normal" (basically, how many have a normal shape and swim appropriately and strongly enough to be able to fertilize an egg). Depending on the situation, you may "produce" the sample at home, or you may need to provide it at the clinic. And yes, since you're undoubtedly wondering at this point: if the collection is done in the clinic, there probably will be a room with some "materials" (read: some nudie magazines from about the time your own father was a teenager) to help you along.

I have to emphasize here: getting a semen analysis is critical. But I understand it can make many men feel hesitant. You're literally having your manhood put under the microscope, which is nerve wracking. I get it; the day my semen analysis results were coming in, I practically had to hide in my office to avoid showing off the gross sweat circles growing under my arms.

But doctors have found the "male-factor," that is, issues with sperm, plays a role in about *half* of all couples going through infertility. Any medical professional working with a couple who is having difficulty conceiving will ensure the man does a full semen workup. View it as your important duty to yourself and your partner—and know that in many cases, if there are any issues with your sperm, there may be treatment options available.

It's also likely you'll have blood work at one or more points to assess your hormone levels and potential chromosomal issues. This can help the doctor understand whether there may be additional factors at play affecting your sperm quality. Other blood tests will likely look at your genetics, helping to figure out whether there are potential variations in your chromosomes that could make it more challenging for you and your partner to produce embryos that implant and grow successfully. This can also reveal whether you and your partner may be more likely to pass on certain genetic diseases. For instance, my background is French Canadian and Olivia is Jewish. Both of our populations have a higher likelihood of carrying Tay-Sachs, a disease that causes damage to nerve cells in the brain and spinal cord. Our blood tests let us rest assured that we did not carry markers for Tay-Sachs.

That said, there may be additional testing you need to undergo if the initial semen analysis reveals a low count or other abnormalities. If there are more challenging issues, it may require further ultrasound or perhaps even a testicular biopsy to look at tissue samples and assess what is causing the issues. It's possible you could also have blockages in your testicular tissue, vas deferens, or elsewhere along the path sperm take toward ejaculation. We'll discuss this and other potential diagnoses pertaining to both you and your partner in greater depth in chapter 5.

Your partner's testing will almost certainly be more complex. It generally involves, at a bare minimum, blood tests to look at the levels of various hormones to get an overall sense of her reproductive health, and to glean an idea of the quantity and quality of her egg supply. Your partner may also undergo some ultrasounds or other additional testing to determine things like whether eggs are actually being released at ovulation, whether one or both of her fallopian tubes may have a blockage, whether her uterus is shaped normally, or myriad other potential factors that can make it difficult to conceive.

Some of these tests may require you to accompany her to the doctor's office in order to drive, as they can be painful and cause several hours of discomfort after the test is over. Be as empathetic as possible during this time. Like I said: none of this is easy, but those of us without a womb definitely get the simpler side.

The second step is to review the results of these tests with a doctor you and your partner trust.

If you and your partner have both made it through all of the testing, then it's time to start discussing results and learning more about what's going on, as well as your options for treatment. In chapter 5 we'll take a look at what these tests can reveal, and what the results might mean in terms of potential treatment options.

Before you go on though, pat yourselves on the back and treat yourselves to a nice dinner or other activity. Head to the movies to see something you've been looking forward to, and get the extra large popcorn. Being easy on yourselves and having things to look forward to is incredibly important, as the stress of infertility is real.

And that's why, before we delve into those test results, we're going to take a quick detour and do something men aren't naturally encouraged to do—but channel your inner Mr. Rogers here for a moment, as we talk about...our feelings.

CHAPTER 2

A CHAPTER ABOUT FEELINGS

My buddy and I searched for another beer, anticipating the resinous scent of the hoppy IPA. We went back many years to college, and had enjoyed getting to know craft beer together, even brewing a few batches. Some were fantastic, so much so that we had even (like probably millions of other guys) toyed around with the idea of opening our own brewery once upon a time.

"What do you think for the next one," my friend called, "should we go with this pale ale or try the double IPA? Or switch it up with a stout?"

I mulled over the options. We had some excellent brews, and there was plenty of it to go around. It was New Year's Eve in our white house with the green shutters, and a close group of friends was with us to celebrate. This gathering had become a new tradition since we moved upstate. Though only a few years old, it was something we already treasured. We'd cook too much good food, drink too much craft beer, listen to Christmas records one last time to round out the holidays, and generally have a merry time.

This special time was also a welcome rest after a stressful few months. Olivia and I had been coming to terms with the idea that getting pregnant wasn't coming easily, and knew we'd have to start looking at getting tests and possibly treatment if we didn't get pregnant soon.

The excitement we'd felt at the beginning of trying had mostly dried up. We hadn't given up, but the days leading up to when Olivia's period was supposed to begin were no longer days of anticipation. Instead, we became resigned to the idea that another month had likely passed where we wouldn't be seeing those two lines on a pregnancy test.

"Let's go with the double IPA," I responded.

I cracked it open and took a sip. The bright citrusy scent was irresistible. Someone put the Bing Crosby Christmas Album on. Everything seemed right.

The liquid caught up with me, so I headed upstairs to the bathroom. As I scaled the stairs, I pulled out my phone for a quick scan through social media. I eased into the brief moment of mindless scrolling, as glowing trees and bottles of champagne filled the screen.

Then a post caught my eye. Two hands holding up what looked like a small photo—a mostly black square with a gray, fuzzy, alien-like blob in the middle. It was an ultrasound, held by two close friends. Beneath the photo, the post read "Coming next June: our newest addition!"

I looked at the picture for a beat. The high of the celebratory atmosphere was instantly gone, replaced by spreading tightness in my collarbone. My eyes stung.

We were at a point in our lives where these types of announcements were becoming more and more common. Most of our close friends were married, many in their late 20s and early 30s. The flood of wedding invitations had slowed, so it was inevitable that the flood of baby shower invitations would be the next cycle to start.

But this was the first announcement I'd seen since we really started to grapple with our difficulty trying to conceive. I wanted to be happy for our friends, but I was also jealous, and sad, and angry at myself for not being happy for them. It felt like they had the one thing we wanted and couldn't seem to attain.

I couldn't just walk back downstairs and rejoin the festivities. Not quite yet. I went into our bedroom for a few minutes and laid down in the low light, feeling the stinging in my eyes and tightness in my chest.

~ ~ ~

As I've said, infertility can be a very lonely journey. No one expects to go through it, and too often, those who do are uncomfortable sharing what they're going through. The truth is, while the causes and treatments for infertility are primarily physical, the most difficult aspect of the journey is dealing with the stress that it causes. In fact, a 1993 research article by Dr. Alice Domar and others showed that women going through infertility experience anxiety and depression levels similar to those in individuals diagnosed with cancer.

You probably already know a bit (or perhaps a lot) about the stress that infertility can produce. And for men, this can feel much harder to admit or grapple with. As I explained earlier, we're often taught that the proper reaction to feelings of stress or anxiety is to keep busy, or to try to fix things and take control. Even worse, society and the media often send the message that it's not "proper" or "manly" for men to express if they're feeling sad or overwhelmed.

These are issues that would require a longer book than this one to sort out, but here's the main thing I want you to know: unless you're already a Zen master, **going through infertility will cause both you and your partner to feel stressed and anxious, which is normal and OK. There is nothing wrong with having those feelings, and there are many different ways to help manage them.**

That's why I felt it was important to include discussion throughout the book to help you make sense of what's going on with you, with your partner, and offer a few ideas for how to take care of both of you.

Now of course, if you or your partner are experiencing stress, anxiety, or depression that is interfering with your everyday life, seek the support of a counselor or therapist right away. But the most important step to managing these feelings is to understand what they are, understand they are normal, and think through some small steps you can take to support yourself and your partner.

How You Might Be Feeling

Accepting that you and your partner are having trouble conceiving can rock your world. Most of us assume that when we want to have kids, we'll have a "normal" experience like we see on TV and the movies—we'll start trying and a few months later we'll be hugging our partner celebrating that positive pregnancy test. We spend years picturing this in our heads, which is why it's such a shock when this doesn't play out.

Remember: feeling upset, anxious, or stressed is normal given that something you have thought about for years and assumed would just happen is now not working. Your life's plans have been totally upended. If one of your good friends had their boss tell them they were going to be promoted in six months, kept talking to them about the great new position and salary they would receive, and then suddenly told him at the end of that six months that he wasn't going to be promoted after all...you'd expect your friend to feel a little upset, right? Well, then you certainly can be expected to be upset when trying to conceive doesn't go to plan.

Here are a few things you might be feeling at the onset of your infertility experience, although this is not a complete list by any means. Remember—all of these are totally normal. It doesn't mean they are pleasant, but feeling these things doesn't make you crazy or a failure—it simply means you are normal.

- Angry at the situation
  - You might find yourself cursing the universe, or God (or whatever your chosen higher power might be), or just cursing in general for being in such a difficult spot. You might wonder what you've done to deserve this difficulty when others seem to have no issue having children.
- Jealous of other couples who are expecting
  - Like me on New Year's Eve, you might find yourself feeling very jealous of couples who are expecting, and also possibly guilty about feeling jealous!
- Sad at the thought of not having children
  - You might start thinking about the things you most envisioned doing with kids (for me, that meant playing piano with them, going to the playground, traveling, and reading books to them before bed) and feel deeply sad, wondering if you will ever get to have that experience.
- Stressed about the unknown of treatments
  - You may particularly worry about your own semen analysis and the possibility the issue has to do with you. You may also worry about what your partner may have to go through in terms of treatments, and wonder how you'll be able to support her.
- Worried and constantly reviewing worst-case scenarios
  - Sometimes stress can get us stuck in a loop of envisioning worst case scenarios. We think by anticipating everything that might go wrong, perhaps we can figure out plans to avoid those things. In reality, this mostly just puts us in

an even more negative mindset and raises our anxiety further.

- Overwhelmed about paying for possible treatments
  - This can be a big one, especially since many men have a deeply ingrained belief that we have to be the provider and the one to "figure things out" financially.
- Generally feeling less "manly"
  - Finally, you might just feel a hard to pin down, nagging sense that somehow you are less "manly" because you can't "get your wife pregnant." Remember the section above on sperm health: while there are some things we can do to take some control over this, there are lots of genetic and environmental factors that we can't fully control.

HOW YOUR PARTNER MIGHT BE FEELING

As you'd expect, almost all of the above also applies to your partner (except of course "feeling less manly.") In addition though, here are some things that your partner may be feeling at these earlier stages of your infertility journey.

- Feeling like her body is "failing"/something is "wrong" with her
  - Women experiencing infertility can feel their body is failing them and that not being able to succeed in a basic function they are "supposed" to be able to carry out means something is "wrong" with them at a deep level.

- Feeling like this might be a sign that she isn't meant to be a mom
    - This may be strongly connected to the first feeling that something is "failing"—i.e., if her body isn't "working" to support a pregnancy, then that might lead to a feeling that she doesn't "deserve" children or isn't "cut out" to be a mother.
- Blaming herself for her diet, weight, body type, etc
    - Just as society does a terrible job supporting men in understanding and expressing their feelings, society sends horribly damaging messages to women about their bodies. Because of this, your partner might feel the infertility is because she isn't "the right weight", or isn't "the right body type", and so forth.

~ ~ ~

I strolled through the meat section, trying to remember what meals we had planned for the week. Was it roast chicken, or tacos? Or both? I had pulled one of my classic moves, forgetting the grocery list in the car. Too lazy to go get it in the upstate New York winter, I wandered the store trying to remember everything.

Truth be told, I didn't mind. I find strange satisfaction in grocery shopping. I always have. Even as a little kid, getting to ride in the cart through the grocery store was one of my favorite things—especially watching the multicolored cereal boxes whiz by.

Unable to remember the meal plan, I grabbed both a chicken and some ground turkey and chucked both in the cart. If we didn't use one, we could freeze it for later.

I steered the cart toward the coffee and tea aisle, nearly done. Then I stopped in my tracks.

A third of the way down the aisle, a woman lingered in the tea section. As she craned her neck to look at some labels on the top shelf and shifted back and forth, I saw the outline of her flowy green sweater draped over her enormous, beach-ball round midsection. She was extremely, extremely pregnant.

I cursed under my breath and swung my cart around, re-routing toward the dairy section to grab eggs. Hopefully by the time I returned to the coffee, she'd have moved on.

~ ~ ~

HOW TO TAKE CARE OF YOURSELF

As you can tell from just these short lists, infertility can do a number on us. The strategies below can help manage those feelings. Not every strategy works for everyone—but pick a couple and get started. Give it a few weeks, and see how you feel!

- Get some physical activity
    - Whether lifting weights, going for a run, doing a yoga class or YouTube video, or taking a walk around your neighborhood, having a regular form of exercise will really help keep you feeling in balance. The most important thing is to pick something you enjoy doing; there's no need to enlist in a high-impact interval training class if you'd rather swim or jog.

- Remind yourself that feelings are just feelings—they're not the truth
    - Feelings are powerful things; they can dominate our existence. But they're not the truth. Take an example of one of the feelings above: that experiencing infertility means we're not cut out to be a father. We may feel this, but that doesn't mean it's true. Your dedication to pursuing parenthood despite the challenge actually demonstrates the strength of your commitment to being a father!
- Remind yourself that making a child and raising a child are two different things
    - This may seem obvious, but passing on your genes has NOTHING to do with being a good father. Not even a little. There are plenty of men out there with healthy reproductive organs and high sperm counts who are not there to support their biological kids in the ways they need them most. Conversely, there are men who become fathers through adoption, fostering, donor sperm, or who just serve as dedicated mentors (think of a coach or teacher), who provide the caring support and unwavering belief necessary to raise a child into a fulfilled and happy adult. Making a child and raising a child are two entirely separate jobs.
- Define for yourself what it means to be a great father
    - Think of the person or people who most exemplify to you what it means to be a great father. What qualities do they have that make them seem "fatherly" in your eyes? My guess is you'll be thinking of qualities like "being supportive" and "sharing things they're passionate about

with their kids," and not things like "had the highest sperm count" or "maintained emotional distance from their kids."

- Do something to clear your mind
    - Do something every day to help clear your mind—this can be as simple as listening to a 5-minute guided meditation, or closing your eyes and setting a timer for 10 minutes and doing some slow deep breathing to take a quick break. This can feel a bit awkward at first, so you may find you need to actually tell yourself "it's ok to take this time for a break."
- Write down how you're feeling
    - Simply writing your feelings down can feel like a nice decluttering for your mind. This doesn't have to take long, again—set a timer for 5 minutes and bullet out some of the things you're thinking about or feeling. And you don't have to show what you write to anyone.
- Research, but don't obsess
    - It can be easy to obsess and constantly search for extra bits of information; you might feel like "if I just read that one additional web page or article, maybe it will be where I find something really important!" It's good to learn more about fertility treatments and the process, but limit how much time you spend to avoid going down a rabbit hole.
- Treat yourself
    - It could be a nice pack of craft beer, a trip to your favorite bookstore, tickets to a game, or a new video game you've been looking at. Make it reasonable and

affordable of course, but don't forget that you're going through something really challenging, and it's ok to do things to help you feel good.

- Try a mantra
    - I know this may sound silly, but having a mantra doesn't have to be super woo-woo. Mantras are really just phrases we think about to help focus ourselves. After all, we train our brain just like any other muscle—if we spend most of our time thinking and wondering about what fertility treatment is going to be like or what we'll do if it doesn't work, we can quickly get into a really negative headspace. Instead, just say some simple, positive things to yourself anytime you have a free moment. Here are some suggestions to start:
        - *"I am strong, and ready to be a father."*
        - *"I am supporting myself and my partner as we work to become parents."*
        - *"It's ok to feel upset. We're going through something really hard."*
        - *"I'm going to remember to go easy on myself."*
- Talk to someone
    - There's an old saying: "A problem shared is a problem halved." As I mentioned earlier, sharing what you're experiencing can be one of the most powerful ways to lighten the burden of the challenges of infertility. Telling a friend, faith leader, or therapist/counselor can really help.

THE WILD WORLD OF INTERNET SEARCHES

As I mentioned earlier, my habit of excessive internet searching to try to cram every bit of available information about infertility was a real thorn in my side at certain points. As with everything about the internet, it can be an amazing resource, and also a repository of unbelievable amounts of dubious information ranging from the innocuous to the out-and-out insane. Here's a quick window into what the experience can be like...

- What you type into the search bar: "Ways to boost sperm health"
    - *First search result:* "THE AMAZING SUPER SPERM SECRET FOUND IN THE DEEP AMAZON RAINFOREST...STRONGER SPERM GUARANTEED IN JUST 30 DAYS!"
        - *Your brain:* "Well that's tempting...wait a minute, it's $129.95 for a month's supply? And there's no list of ingredients?" *Sketched out by the incessant popup windows pushing you to BUY NOW, you close the tab*
    - *Second search result:* "Article from the British Journal on Sperm Health: The Effects of Beta-Phospholipid Alpha-4 Proteinase Supplementation on Spermatazoa Among the Male Population of Southeast London Between the Years 1956 and 1958"
        - *Your brain:* *Seizes up* "Uh...I can't even understand the title, let alone the content. Could be useful, but I need something a bit simpler..."

  - *Third search result:* "North Dakota Man's Sperm Count Skyrockets After Eating Nothing But Boiled Cabbage for Three Years"
    - Your brain: "CRAP, I NEVER EAT BOILED CABBAGE! Wait, hold on. Get a grip, Keegan. No…just no…"
  - *Fourth search result:* "Four Simple Changes to Improve Sperm Health: Recommendations from RESOLVE: The National Infertility Association"
    - Your brain: "Ok, this looks promising. It's from a real, reputable organization, and in plain English." *CLICK*

You get the point! Be a smart consumer, take things on the internet with a grain of salt, and try to avoid information overload.

HOW TO TAKE CARE OF YOUR PARTNER

It's so important to be a supportive partner during this journey. Your partner is almost certainly just as anxious, stressed, and worried as you are, and it can be hard to know what to say or do. The list of things below should help you get started. Maybe even show the list to your partner and ask which one she would appreciate you focusing on!

- Communicate
  - It's ok to be strong, but being silent can weaken your partnership during infertility. Make time to talk about how you're both feeling, what supports you need more or less of, and about your hopes for the future. This level of openness will be key to staying united no matter what path your journey to parenthood takes, and can help you

recommit regularly to why you wanted to have a baby to begin with.

- Remind your partner of the qualities she has that will make her a great mother
  - Just as it's important to define for yourself the qualities that make a great father, your partner may feel she's somehow not meant for motherhood. You've obviously decided your partner would be a good mother for your future kids. What qualities of hers let you know that? Tell her about them!
- Listen, don't fix
  - With infertility, there usually isn't a quick or easy fix. In my case, this meant I needed to practice something Olivia was more naturally skilled at: just listening. There's no need to react or suggest a solution. Just listen. At the end it's ok to simply say: "I can tell you're really upset. I'm sorry that you feel that way. I love you and am here for you."
- Attend appointments as much as possible, particularly discussions with the doctor
  - While you may not need to go to every single brief blood draw monitoring appointment, you should certainly attend as many appointments as you can, and make a special effort to attend any appointments that involve discussions with the doctor about planning treatments, debriefing treatments, and so forth.
- Plan fun non-baby related things to enjoy and look forward to
  - Life during infertility can seem like everything revolves around trying to have a baby. Intentionally plan to do

things that are NOT baby-related in any way, whether it's going for a hike, heading to the movies, or planning an adults-only dinner party or barbecue.

- Don't put off all your plans
    - You and your partner may find yourselves saying "Well, we shouldn't schedule that trip/big family party/other thing we've been talking about in case we're doing fertility treatments/pregnant/etc." When you get farther into treatment, sure, you may want to avoid major plans in a particular month. In general though, plan that trip, or buy those concert tickets! You need and deserve things to look forward to.
- Show gratitude
    - Showing gratitude is one of the most important things for any relationship, so let your partner know how much you appreciate her. Challenge yourself for a week to thank your partner out loud once per day for something she does (as big as working to have a baby, or as small as folding the laundry!). You'll be amazed at how powerful this small act can be.
- Treat your partner
    - This doesn't have to be something really extravagant—it can be as simple as stopping on the way home to get one of those nice artisanal chocolate bars she loves.

Building a Support Team

"I really appreciate you making time to talk. I'm excited about your story and how important it is to share." The reporter from our local paper looked across our kitchen table as she spoke to us. She had an easy approach to conversation, and I could see the genuine depth of empathy in her eyes.

"Why don't we start at the beginning," she went on. "I think it's important for readers to hear more about you two, how you got together, and how you found out that you'd need to pursue fertility treatments."

Olivia and I glanced at each other. It was like looking in a mirror: we both wore the same eyebrow-raised expression, the corners of our lips slightly turned up in amusement.

"Oh boy," I said with mock exasperation. "Where to start?"

The reporter laughed. "I understand—it must be a long story! How about this: tell me how you met."

Olivia launched into the story of how we met. I'd heard the beats of the story many times (and indeed, had lived it), but always loved reminiscing about it: the first messages on the internet dating site, our explorations around New York City, our shared love of diners. They were sweet memories. Soon the discussion was rolling.

Engaging in a two-hour interview about our infertility journey wasn't how we'd planned to spend our Sunday. A few days prior, I'd penned a letter to the editor noting that it was National Infertility Awareness Week. That same afternoon, the editor called and asked if we'd be willing to expand on our story for a full feature in the paper. The call was so unexpected that I sputtered for a few seconds before managing to thank them and say I'd have to discuss it with Olivia.

"So…guess who called as I was leaving work," I said as I entered the house that night.

"Uh…who?"

"The editor from the paper! They want to write a whole article about our infertility journey. Isn't that nuts?"

Olivia did a double take. "What? Really? Just because of that letter you wrote?"

"Apparently! They said they thought it was a really important issue and wanted a full story to go with the letter to the editor. But I mean…this is the paper. Thousands of people read it! I don't know about having a full story. Plus anyone could see it online."

I rubbed my forehead, grappling with the thought of "coming out" so visibly. At this point, most of our close family knew what we were going through, but we hadn't really shared what we were going through beyond that circle. I had visions of walking into the restaurant in our village and people nudging each other and pointing at us, whispering about "that poor couple who can't have kids."

"I know," she said, "the thought of thousands of people reading our whole story is…a little intimidating. We might find out about other people going through it though."

"That's true, and who knows? It could help someone else who's just starting this crazy journey," I responded.

~ ~ ~

Now that you have some ideas of how to support yourself and your partner, I'd recommend both you and your partner consider reaching out to some trusted people who could be a support team for the path ahead. Like many other couples, it took Olivia and me a long time to be comfortable sharing our fertility struggles. If you'd told us we'd end up having an article in our local paper about our infertility earlier in our journey, we'd have laughed in your face.

I later realized how common it is for couples to feel hesitant about sharing what they're going through. And why wouldn't it be? Think about the list above of things you and your partner might be feeling: angry, sad, jealous, overwhelmed, like a "failure." These are messy feelings, and no one likes to share messy feelings. It can feel as if we're unfairly burdening others with our problems. Depending on your family and culture, you may also feel like it is not "normal" to talk about problems, particularly around fertility.

Yet despite how hard it is to talk about infertility, it is one of the most important things that can make your experience easier. The point isn't necessarily to seek advice (though if you trust their advice all the better)—it's simply to feel heard.

Having a support person or team gives an external place for you and your partner to talk through your feelings and reactions to what's happening, which can also be a huge help for your relationship. Olivia and I certainly noticed this; during the first 8-10 months of our infertility, we basically only had each other to talk to. We communicated frequently and openly which was positive, but I was surprised at how relieving it was when we first shared what was happening with a small group of family and friends. It was a subtle shift, but suddenly it felt like this difficult experience wasn't just "ours" anymore. Suddenly, we had a team of supporters on our side.

Here are some options you may want to consider to build your support team, and some considerations to help you decide what is best:

One possible option is to tell family members. This depends on your relationships, and every family comes with its own dynamics. Consider who you'd trust and what you'd say if they ask if they can share with anyone else in the family. Be clear on your boundaries here—if you don't want them to share, say so explicitly.

A few possible reasons that telling family members can be helpful: First, it may relieve existing pressure and questions about your plans for a little one. Every family has a member who loves to needle the younger couples, asking about when "the stork" might be coming, dropping subtle hints about how "it would be so nice to have another baby in the family" or perhaps, throwing all subtlety to the wind and asking in the middle of a holiday dinner: "WHEN ARE YOU HAVING A BABY?" You already know these questions are downright unbearable. Revealing what you're going through may help stem them. And note: people are much more likely to ask the woman these questions, so if you think no one is asking these questions, double check with your partner.

Second, sharing with family can be helpful because you may discover any history of infertility; this could be valuable information for your doctor. We already knew that Olivia's grandmother had several miscarriages and difficult periods, hereditary information which was helpful to share. We also learned about some other family members on both sides who struggled to conceive or experienced pregnancy losses. Even if the information doesn't necessarily have bearing on your particular case, knowing this can help you feel less alone and open up chances to bond with family members who've been in your shoes.

Another option is to tell a friend or friends. You are likely at an age when many other friends are starting families. Well-meaning comments or questions about whether you're next can sting. Letting a friend or two know can stifle such inquiries and may also lead you to find others who are experiencing, or have experience, the same struggles.

But this can be challenging for men in particular. Society's portrayal of male friendships often focuses on physical activities like sports, or on a stereotypical view in which our conversations stay at the surface level and avoid deeper feelings. In contrast, portrayals of female friends in media often highlight vivid, emotional conversations. These stereotypes have real effects, so it's normal to feel that sharing this with one of your buddies may be "overstepping" or "too real".

To make this easier, think about a way you can share what's happening that feels manageable to you. The goal is just to start the conversation and share what's happening—it may lead to a heart-to-heart, but the important thing is to take the first step.

You don't need to make a big thing of it—you can simply suggest a usual activity like going to the driving range, or for a beer, or a hike. Wait for a natural moment, and plan what you want to say in advance. Here are some suggestions for ways you might open the conversation:

- "So Olivia and I are thinking of starting a family. I'm excited to be a dad, but we've been trying for a bit with no luck yet."
- "I saw that (insert mutual friend name here) is going to be a dad. We're actually trying too. No pregnancy yet though, I'm just hoping it happens soon."

Even if your friend just nods and says "that really sucks," you've still made a big step in sharing. It will become easier, and you're set up to return more naturally to the conversation next time you get together.

If you're not yet comfortable sharing what's going on with family or friends, that's OK too. You still have some great options available that can help you find a team for support.

This brings us to another option, consulting with a trusted faith/spiritual advisor, a counselor, or a coach. Taking this route can be really helpful, as all of these people are trained and experienced in providing advice around life's challenges. If you practice a particular faith, speaking to your priest/pastor/rabbi/etc. not only provides a venue to share what's happening, it can also help you navigate how your own beliefs might play into decisions and discussions as you and your partner plan potential treatment. Therapists, counselors, and coaches (the "life coach" kind), can serve the same external ear to listen and provide helpful advice.

Regardless of which of the options above sound best, starting to build a support team will make your journey seem easier. Reaching out and asking for help is not something that comes easily to most men given what society "expects" of us. View this as an opportunity to build a new muscle. Not only will it help in your journey, it will also prepare you to be a better father!

~ ~ ~

Our story was set to go in the paper in the following Thursday's edition. We rushed home from work that day, eager but nervous to see it in print. I beat Olivia home by a few minutes and waited by the mailbox for her. When she finally pulled in, she stopped partway up the driveway, didn't even turn the car off, and hurried toward me.

I slowly pulled the folded paper out of the mailbox. As I unfurled it, we both gasped.

Our story, and a picture of us the reporter had taken, was on the very top of the front page. The lead story for the week.

"Holy crap," I stammered.

"Well, there's no hiding now," Olivia mused.

After reading the story from start to end and crying multiple times at the beautiful way the reporter had rendered it, we headed off for our evening walk. As we came to the center of town, I suggested we pop into the wine store.

Roberta, the owner, waved and smiled. It was nice to live in a small village where the people who owned the shops were our neighbors. I wandered down the shelves looking for something suitable for the chilly fall evening.

As I pondered the relative merits of an $8 bottle versus a $10 bottle of Spanish red, a voice piped up behind me.

"Keegan?"

It was Jim, a neighbor down the street. I smiled. We'd always exchanged little pleasantries over the years, chatting about the weather, the news, or more frequently, our greyhound Desmond, who loved to stop every neighbor for a dose of pets and ear scratches.

"Jim, how are you?"

"Good. Hey, I just wanted to say—it was really brave of you guys to have that article written."

I tensed slightly. I knew we'd hear from neighbors about the article, but didn't expect it so soon! Olivia had overheard and moved closer to join.

"You know," Jim continued, "my wife and I went through the same thing 25 years ago. Miscarriages, failed IVF cycles. It was horrible. We were lucky to adopt two wonderful boys, but those stories don't get told enough. Thanks for being courageous enough to put it out there. I think it will help people."

We continued to talk to Jim for a few minutes more, instantly bonded by the shared battle. After parting, we checked out with my $8 bottle of Spanish red, and left the store to walk home. The chill of early fall had set in, but our discussion with Jim left us feeling warm.

"I think we made the right choice," said Olivia as we strolled up our street.

I smiled. "I think so too. I guess we're going to be the local infertility celebrity couple now?"

~ ~ ~

BUILD HABITS, BUILD STRENGTH, AND BE KIND TO YOURSELF

Hopefully you're already thinking about which of the ideas from this chapter might work for you. You don't have to come out to the world in your local newspaper by any means, but the great thing about trying strategies to support yourself and your partner, and reaching out to build a support team, is that they can become habits that strengthen your relationship in the long run. I don't think Olivia and I ever considered at the outset of our long and winding path to parenthood that it could actually make us a stronger couple and better parents, but years later, thanks to lots of work and communication, we feel closer than ever before. Both of us had times when we felt like we were totally burnt out and ready to give up, but we learned it was normal and OK to feel that way, and we learned and practiced strategies to help.

These habits also built a sense of kindness and understanding which was of particular use during the hardest times in our journey. This may be the most important thing to emerge from these efforts. Infertility gives you ample opportunity to blame yourself, blame each other, and to give in to anger and anxiety.

However, if you practice the habits above, you'll start building a reserve of kindness toward yourself and your partner which will help you choose to stop, breathe, care for yourselves, and remember why you're going through this crazy journey in the first place: to become wonderful, loving parents.

CHAPTER 3

FOUR FACTORS TO HELP YOU CHOOSE A CLINIC

The number of tabs on our internet browser was multiplying like a rampant wildfire. We were deep into research mode, analyzing every bit of data we could find on the two fertility clinics in our area. We had tabs with CDC data, tabs with FertilityIQ reviews, tabs with random other reviews from other sites, and even blogs we'd found where people mentioned the clinics and their experiences at them.

Clinic A was a relatively large travel clinic with nearly a dozen doctors listed on its website, serving thousands of patients from around the country each year, and with several outposts around the state and country. Clinic B was smaller, part of a regional network of fertility clinics, with three doctors listed on its website and serving a couple hundred patients per year.

My eyes glazed over. "Alright, well this is a lot of information. They both take our insurance, thank goodness. What do you think?" I asked Olivia.

"Ugh," she sighed. "I mean the overall live birth rate for Clinic B is a little higher than for Clinic A, but this data is old and they have completely different doctors working there now."

"Yeah," I responded, switching between tabs, scanning the information for the umpteenth time. "All the reviews for Clinic B seem to talk about the prior doctor. I wish there were more mentions of the new doctors."

"On the other hand," she went on, "Clinic A just has a lot of clients. Its website and facilities look really fantastic, but some of the reviews make it sound like...well, a factory or something. I'd rather see the same doctor and nurses consistently."

"That's true," I nodded. "And I mean, there are a few reviews for the new doctors at Clinic B and they seem decent. There are some bad reviews too, but a lot of them are people who didn't get pregnant. I imagine that's hard, so I kind of take them with a grain of salt. And Clinic A's reviews are all over the place. Some people swear by them, others say they went one round and then got out of there. So...what do you think?"

Olivia pondered for a second.

"What's most important to me is having a more personal feel. I know Clinic A looks really well-equipped, but I just feel in my gut that Clinic B's smaller size is the way to go."

I couldn't argue with her reasoning.

"Alright then," I nodded. "I'll make an appointment."

~ ~ ~

The Four Factors in Choosing a Clinic: Cost, Convenience, Reputation, and Compatibility

We were fortunate in our search for an IVF clinic. Not only did we have two nationally reputable clinics in our area, we had insurance that provided partial coverage for treatments and for required medications. Even with such a favorable position, it took lots of thinking and research to decide which clinic and doctor was right for us.

In the end, we found four factors that really matter. First is *cost.* While cost doesn't necessarily reflect quality, it's a critical consideration for most couples. Second is *convenience*—fertility treatment is physically taxing, so finding a location that works for you and your partner is important. *Reputation* is third. It's easy to find information about different clinics through social media, online reviews, and publicly available statistics. Finally, there's *compatibility*, which means both the clinic's suitability to your particular situation, and also the degree to which you feel the doctors, nurses, and staff meld with your personality and preferences. In this chapter, we'll consider these four factors and provide recommendations and resources to help you make the best decision for you and your partner.

My hope is you have at least a couple of good options available to you, as we did. But depending on your location, insurance situation, and the particulars of your infertility diagnosis, you may be more constrained. There are plenty of couples who drive three hours (or more) to a fertility clinic because it's the closest and best option. If that's where you're at, know I'm rooting especially hard for you.

Getting the Lay of the Land: Your Fertility Treatment Clinic Options

Before looking more closely at the four factors, let's look at the general landscape of fertility clinics. Fertility treatment is a rapidly growing field of medicine, and the good news is the number of clinics and providers have increased greatly in recent years.

- Treatment from regular OB/GYN

First, your partner's typical OB/GYN office may offer some interventions that could help with certain types of infertility. At the very least, the OB/GYN should offer testing and diagnoses including blood work and possibly some ultrasounds to help assess the situation. Additionally, the OB/GYN may be able to prescribe medications to help with certain issues (for instance, ones to support ovulation such as letrozole or Clomid).

For some couples, this level of support may be all that is necessary. In fact, we have friends who tried for several years to get pregnant, and were ultimately able to do so because the woman's OB/GYN discovered she was not ovulating. With medication to promote ovulation and timed intercourse, they now have two healthy children.

One caveat here—while we've come a long way from the old days where the only advice doctors could give a couple was to "keep on trying," knowledge of infertility varies among OB/GYN providers and clinics. Many clinics do great work, even partnering with fertility specialists to conduct ongoing education for their staff. That said, some OB/GYN providers or nurses or staff may not be as well-informed about fertility issues. Your partner may wish to ask the OB/GYN or nurses if they have any partnerships with fertility clinics or specific professional learning opportunities about treatments for fertility issues.

Hopefully you'll find (or have already found) one of the outstanding medical teams who can help you and your partner understand what's going on and make a plan, and perhaps even offer some treatment options. Just remember the following advice: If your partner and you do not feel like you're getting answers to your questions, or like your concerns are not being heard or are being dismissed, don't hesitate to seek another opinion or find another medical provider. Advocating for yourselves is important, and ensures you have the best shot at success.

- Fertility clinics

If your path is like ours, you'll move from the regular OB/GYN to the big guns: a dedicated fertility clinic. According to the CDC, as of 2019, there were roughly 500 fertility clinics around the US, with more opening all the time. High-quality fertility treatment is more accessible than it has ever been. Yet there are still limits; most full-service clinics are clustered in or near mid-to-large size cities, and more rural areas often do not have dedicated fertility providers.

The burgeoning number of providers means that the types and sizes of clinics varies. To help you make sense of things as you start your research, here are a few things to look at to help you assess what type of clinic might be right for you and your partner.

First, *get an idea of the size of the clinic*. There are several ways to do this. You can start by visiting the clinic's website to get a sense of how many doctors, nurses, and laboratory staff they have. Some clinics may only have one doctor, while larger clinics may list a number of providers. The number of providers doesn't necessarily indicate anything about quality, but if having a consistent relationship with a single doctor is important to you and your partner, you'll want to ask whether you'll see the same doctor each time you visit.

Another way to assess the size is to look at the CDC's database of information about clinics (https://www.cdc.gov/art/artdata/index.html). This website is a treasure trove of information. The site is easy to navigate, but to assess size, go to the specific clinic's page and look for the *total number of cycles* (note the data lags by a couple of years, usually the most recent complete and available data is from 1-2 years ago). You'll see the number of cycles completed varies widely from clinic to clinic, ranging from several dozen to several thousand. There are different reasons for this variation: some clinics with fewer cycles may serve a highly specialized population, such as couples with particularly challenging cases, while other clinics with fewer cycles may just have fewer doctors or be in a less populated area.

Again, this doesn't really indicate anything about quality, but it does help you understand the types of questions you may want to investigate as you research what clinic is right for you. For instance, you may want to ask a smaller clinic if they have a particular specialty area.

The next thing you'll want to understand is *whether the doctors (called reproductive endocrinologists or REs) perform all treatments.* In some clinics, there may be nurses, nurse practitioners, midwives, certified nurse midwives, physician's assistants, and other providers. While the surgical components of IVF such as an egg retrieval and embryo transfer are performed by the doctor/RE, other treatments such as IUIs may be performed by other qualified staff such as nurse practitioners or registered nurses. While this is a normal practice, the information may be important to you and your partner.

Another aspect to research is *whether the clinic provides any related health and wellness services* such as counseling, acupuncture, or nutrition classes. Some people find wellness supports helpful as part of their fertility treatment. If you or your partner are interested in these services, you'll want to know whether the clinic offers any in-house, or perhaps has associated or recommended providers who work in alignment with their treatment schedules.

You'll also want to understand *whether the clinic serves mostly local clients, or if they are open to/billed as a clinic for travel clients.* This is worth noting because there are a growing number of fertility clinics offering high-volume care at lower out-of-pocket cost by serving a large number of travel clients, many of whom fly into the location of the clinic for certain parts of treatment. As wild as this may sound, paying the cost of an airplane ticket and hotel plus treatment at these higher-volume clinics can, in some cases, still be less expensive than pursuing local treatment, particularly in areas where there are few fertility providers.

I know I sound like a broken record, but the business model and clientele also don't indicate much about quality of care. Travel clinics serve a real need, and until we hit a point where infertility treatment becomes more broadly accessible and affordable, they are filling a niche in the market and helping thousands of people become parents.

This leads to the last thing you'll want to understand, which is *whether the clinic provides all treatments and monitoring, or whether the clinic is part of a larger network in which you conduct local monitoring and travel farther for more intensive parts of treatment such as an IVF egg retrieval.* This can be more convenient, as it cuts down on travel for you given the high level of monitoring involved in many treatments, which may require blood work and ultrasound every day or two. That said, just know it may mean you have to travel to another clinic for some parts of the treatment. This may not be an issue for you, but you'll want to know this up front.

- International Clinics

International clinics, such as those based in Mexico, Barbados, the Czech Republic, India, or Thailand, may also be an option to consider, particularly if you do not have insurance coverage for fertility treatments. Medical treatment in countries like the United States, Canada, and the United Kingdom can be quite costly, and some couples find that pursuing IVF abroad can be less expensive in total, even with the cost of travel and accommodations included. Many of these clinics provide the same high-quality care and treatment you'd find at a clinic in your own state.

While the choices around international clinics and treatment are too numerous to cover in depth here, it could be another great option to consider.

All of this information should give you the general lay of the land. Ultimately, this combined with the other four factors of cost, convenience, reputation, and compatibility will help you make the right decision for you.

Cost: The Bottom Line

I won't sugar coat this: cost may be the single most important factor for many couples pursuing fertility treatments. Whether or not you have insurance coverage (and what clinics accept that insurance coverage if you do have it) can whittle down your options significantly.

Don't be discouraged if this is the case. First, know you're being a smart future parent by making a sound economic choice. Raising kids is an additional cost, and considering what is most affordable for you will help you be in a better financial position to become parents. Second, remember there are many wonderful options available these days for high-quality care. A clinic that charges more for their IVF cycles is not necessarily better than one with a lower sticker price. Ultimately, you can find people who have received care from every single fertility clinic out there who have found success, and people who went to the same clinic who have not.

Convenience: How Far Do You Want to Go?

Given how involved fertility treatments can be, convenience of accessibility and location are important. If you're fortunate to be in an area with several clinics, you might consider whether a clinic that is farther from your house is a better fit than a closer one. In this case, it's likely the other factors such as compatibility or cost may be most critical to you.

On the other hand, you may not live close to any clinics. In this case, you may be considering whether flying to one of the clinics specializing in travel clients might be a better option than a clinic which is drivable but still far. Whether flying or facing a lengthy drive, you'll have to drill down on the convenience factor. My recommendation here is to ask clinics how they work with traveling clients' schedules and what their expectations are. Clinics should be able to give you an idea of which appointments you absolutely must go to in person versus where they can work to help coordinate blood work, ultrasounds, and other monitoring with a provider closer to home.

Something helpful in making these determinations around convenience is hearing other patient's experiences—which brings us to the third factor.

REPUTATION: THE JOYS OF THE INTERNET AGE

Love it or hate it, the internet has made it easy to find out what other people think about anything imaginable. While your Uncle Arnold's opinions on politics or the latest TV shows may not be useful, other people's experiences with services like fertility clinics can provide some information to help decide what's best for you and your partner.

As with everything else on the internet, take the information with a grain of salt, and focus on factual information. Use multiple sources and look for trends. Remember the yo-yo? Most of the reviews you find online were probably written at one of the extreme ups or downs of infertility. Indeed, you'll notice that reviews generally filter into two camps: people who are thrilled because they had a baby after going to a clinic, and people who are disappointed because they did not find success at the clinic. You already know how emotionally difficult it is to go through infertility, so look across many reviews to get an overall sense of what patients' experience is like.

In addition, look to other sources online to assess reputation. Two great sources are: Fertility IQ (fertilityiq.com) and the CDC website (linked earlier). Fertility IQ's website has an entire section dedicated to doctor/clinic ratings, which contain detailed answers from verified patients to questions like "During treatment, were you treated more like a human or a number at the clinic?" and "What's one piece of advice you would give a prospective patient for this clinic?" It's one of the most comprehensive databases of fertility doctor and clinic reviews, so it's a great first stop. As a bonus, Fertility IQ also has loads of other great resources such as videos and courses on various aspects of fertility treatment. Just remember: all patient reviews, though verified, are still only expressions of one person's opinion.

The CDC website is a great companion to Fertility IQ and other online reviews because it is 100% objective and based on hard data alone. Once you select a given clinic on the CDC website, you'll find a landing page for each one with helpful basic information such as what type of infertility services they provide and the total number of cycles performed in a given year.

The page has several tabs or sections at the top. One is called "Patient and Cycle Characteristics," where you can find information such as the age range breakdown and diagnoses of patients at the clinic. This can be helpful in determining whether the clinic may serve or specialize in a certain patient population or particular diagnoses. The next tabs, "Success Rates: Patients Using Own Eggs" and "Success Rates: Patients Using Donor Eggs" allow you to look at outcomes for the clinic in many different combinations and formulations, such as "What was the percentage of actual egg retrievals that resulted in a live birth?" or "What was the percentage of actual egg retrievals that resulted in singleton (one baby) live births?"

Be forewarned: this site contains a lot of information and you may feel like you need a master's degree in statistics to understand some portions. If it's overwhelming, you can just look at the overall success rates to get a sense of the clinic's outcomes. Take this all in context and remember that fertility treatments are complex. One clinic having a higher percentage of live births per actual egg retrieval does not necessarily mean it is "better" than one with a lower percentage. For instance, one clinic may specialize in serving clients with more challenging cases. That clinic may have a lower percentage of live births than others, but may in fact have far more advanced technology and procedures available to support their clientele with complex treatments most couples do not require.

A side note before moving on to the last factor: absorbing this data can present some challenges for men. Again, society encourages us to take action, research, and fix things. It can be tempting to think that if we just read a few more statistics or reviews, we'll have perfect information and know exactly what to do. But this is an art, not a science. Put all of the information together from your research into the four factors, and trust that you and your partner will make the right decision for you.

COMPATIBILITY: THE X FACTOR

The final factor is compatibility, which boils down to you and your partner answering the question: *What qualities are important to us in a doctor or clinic?* If you've done research into cost, convenience, and reputation, you likely feel much more familiar with the lay of the land. You may have narrowed down a list of several clinics and doctors you're interested in pursuing treatment with.

When you reach this point, I recommend discussing the following questions, which will help you determine the compatibility factors that are most important to you and your partner:

- Is the size of the clinic important to us? If so, do we prefer a larger or smaller clinic? Why?
- What qualities are most important to us in our doctor? In nurses and other staff?

- Is it important for us to have a clinic that offers adjunct services like acupuncture, counseling, or wellness classes?
- How important is "bedside manner"? In other words, do we prefer a doctor/clinical care team that is more supportive and positive, or more direct and realistic?
- If we aren't comfortable with any aspect of the care, or have additional questions or concerns, how will we let each other know?

Knowing the answers to these questions will help in the final step, which is putting the information together about all four factors to determine a clinic to work with. Again, this is an art and not a science; you may get a positive impression about a clinic or doctor from your research, and then get to the first appointment and find you or your partner have concerns about the experience.

~ ~ ~

We pulled into the parking lot of the three-story brick building, several minutes early for our appointment. Elton John crooned on the radio about a yellow brick road. Low clouds slung down across an overcast sky. I wondered if we had entered the wrong address in our maps app—nothing about this unremarkable edifice indicated we had found the IVF clinic. It looked more suited to a vaguely named financial services company.

As we drove around the back, the doors with the clinic's logo etched on them came into view. A man and woman were walking out, their faces a strange mix of weariness and relief. The woman clutched a long white strip that looked like a grocery store receipt in her left hand, which fluttered behind her as she walked. An ultrasound.

A rush of questions ran through my mind: What's the ultrasound showing? Are they pregnant? How did they get pregnant—IUI, IVF, something else? Does that mean this is a great clinic? Maybe this is an omen we're going to get pregnant with the help of this doctor...or maybe if they're pregnant, we won't get pregnant because we have to balance out some great cosmic scale...

"You ready?" Olivia jolted me back to the present.

I was and I wasn't. On one hand, meeting this doctor gave the possibility of hope we'd been missing for so long. On the other hand, we were familiar with the stories of many couples who had been through fertility treatments and knew this initial appointment was only the first step on what could be a long road. Life in the gray zone between hope and fear is the daily reality of infertility.

We stepped out of the car. I grabbed Olivia's hand.

"Here we go."

~ ~ ~

A Final Word: Be Supportive of Your Partner, and Easy on Yourself

As you and your partner decide on where to pursue treatment, try to keep things in perspective and remember there's no such thing as a perfect clinic or perfect doctor. You and your partner are making the best choice you can.

Part of making the best choice you can means being supportive of your partner's desires. You may have strong feelings about the clinic and doctors, and those are valid, but we as men have to remember our partner will be the one bearing the brunt of any potential treatments. If you have some disagreements about important factors, that is OK. However, always lean toward being supportive of your partner in these decisions.

Finally, go easy on yourself. The fertility journey is often a long one, and we as men can get very hung up on fulfilling the role that society often imposes on us to "fix" things and have all the answers. There are no perfect answers, and there are doctors and staff at every fertility clinic who go to work every day trying their best to help people like you and me. If you find yourself obsessing over outcomes data or reviews, give yourself a break and step away. Do some deep breathing, go for a walk, or hit the gym.

Do all of these things, and you and your partner will find the right clinic and doctor for you. Now, it's time to dig in: let's look at some of the most common possible causes of infertility, and then delve into possible treatments.

CHAPTER 4

POTENTIAL DIAGNOSES: WHAT'S THE ROOT CAUSE?

"What do you think the doctor's going to say?" Olivia asked.

I scratched my chin briefly, mentally reviewing what we knew based on the results of the battery of tests and labs from the prior months. After blood work and a saline sonogram of her uterus and fallopian tubes, her regular OBGYN told us everything looked normal. After our initial meeting with the fertility clinic, they ordered more extensive blood work on both of us, and also conducted a semen analysis. My semen analysis had come back—also normal. Now, it was time to meet with the RE and make our treatment plan.

By this point I'd heard countless stories of couples experiencing infertility, so based on what I'd learned, I responded to Olivia's question: "Well, it sounds like there's nothing obviously wrong unless something totally unexpected came up in these tests. So I'm guessing we'll just get the 'unexplained infertility' diagnosis. Which probably means starting IUIs."

She nodded her head. "Yeah, I can't imagine there are any major surprises waiting. Still, I'm nervous."

We were back in the parking lot outside the drab, three-story brick building that housed the fertility clinic. Stepping out of the car, we experienced the climactic whiplash of the thick, humid mid-summer air, immediately followed by the always-a-touch-too-chilly air conditioner blasting within the clinic.

By now, the clinic waiting room was a familiar stop. The light earth-tone walls, the slightly uncomfortable chairs, the constant trickle emanating from a large stone memorial to the clinic's founder, which was mounted on the wall and featured one of those never-ending waterfalls. We settled into a pair of chairs, holding hands, and glanced idly at the pile of magazines.

There was the New York Magazine *I'd already flipped through three times on prior visits, with the cover story on the best restaurants in New York City. It made me think of our carefree days when we lived in Brooklyn, when all we worried about was what neighborhood and restaurant we wanted to explore next. Chinese in Queens? Pizza in South Brooklyn? Pakistani in Jackson Heights? Those days seemed impossibly distant.*

After the usual twenty minute wait, the nurse called us back and ushered us into the doctor's office. From our first appointment, we'd felt quite at home with the RE. She exuded warmth and poise. She was confident enough not to sugar coat how many aspects of fertility treatment are still somewhat mysterious, but always explained her analysis and thinking to us in clear terms. She got down to business reviewing all of our results.

"Based on everything we can see, many of the tests and results are as we would expect. That said, there is one test which stood out to me. Olivia, when you had your AMH tested at your regular OB, did he or she explain that your level is lower than expected for your age?"

I felt her hand tighten—quickly, almost imperceptibly. We glanced at each other, brows furrowed. Fortunately, we'd done our research and knew from the countless articles we'd read and podcasts we'd listened to that AMH levels help measure a woman's egg reserves. Unfortunately, we also knew that having low AMH was not a promising sign.

"No," said Olivia. "The OB said all my hormone levels were normal."

I ever so briefly saw some disappointment flash across the doctor's eyes—not at us, I perceived, but at the original OB. She was a consummate professional, and obviously didn't relish having to contradict another doctor's advice.

"I understand," replied the RE. "Let me share my interpretation of your hormone levels, which can be a little different when looking through the specific lens of infertility. Your AMH is currently 0.98. At your age, we would expect that number to be higher—perhaps in the 2-3 range. Now we always look at everything in the broad context of all of your testing, and we should remember other factors do appear to be normal. That said, this level of AMH suggests to me that you may have some degree of diminished ovarian reserve, or DOR. Have you heard this term or diagnosis before?"

Again, I felt Olivia's hand tighten. I glanced at her and saw a mix of confusion and sadness. A beat passed.

I jumped in: "I think we've heard of DOR, basically a lower number of eggs, correct? Are you sure?"

As the RE explained, I kept glancing briefly at Olivia. Her eyes were moist, reflecting the overhead lights.

"Ultimately I want to make a plan that you're comfortable with and that gives you the best shot at success. With patients who have some degree of diminished ovarian reserve, even if yours may not be severe, my main concern is retrieving sufficient eggs to conceive a viable embryo. So we have a couple of options. First, we could try IUI. Remember every situation is different, but my sense of your odds of success through IUI would be probably in the 5-10% range given what we have learned from testing. Another choice is for us to try IVF. Given your circumstances, the odds of success with IVF would probably be in

the 40-50% range. I know you'll have to consider finances and all of this information. Take your time and we can always reconvene in a few weeks to firm up a treatment plan. I want you to be comfortable with whatever we choose."

We asked a few more cursory questions, thanked the doctor and then moved to a small consultation room to meet with the financial counselor who would help us with insurance. The counselor provided and explained some paperwork and options for either doing IUIs or moving directly to IVF, then gave us a few minutes to talk in private

"I...just didn't expect this. I don't have enough eggs," Olivia said. The moistness in her eyes had turned into an emptiness.

~ ~ ~

The doctor's diagnosis and recommendation were among the many surprising twists along our route to parenthood. In this chapter, we'll delve into information that will prepare you for the conversation I described above: the moment when your testing is over and your medical team provides their best understanding of the issues and a possible diagnosis for your infertility.

I wasn't prepared for how monumental this conversation felt. In the days leading up to it, my heart pounded any time I thought about meeting with the doctor. Reflecting back, this seems natural: we'd been thrown into utter uncertainty around the basic path to procreation. The possibility of understanding why this was happening was a major step toward resolution.

To help you feel prepared, this chapter will provide an overview of common issues testing may reveal. We'll start with issues pertaining to your reproductive apparatus, and then talk about issues pertaining to your partner.

What follows is not meant to provide an exhaustive list of every potential issue with the male and female reproductive systems. My goal here is just to ensure you're well equipped to navigate discussions with your doctor around the majority of common issues that contribute to infertility. There are plenty of other more comprehensive resources out there if you want a deep dive. After the overview, we'll look at how to ensure you get all the important information you need. Let's dive in.

COMMON ISSUES WITH THE MALE REPRODUCTIVE APPARATUS

Plentiful normal and motile sperm are our primary contribution to the conception equation. Hence, most reproductive issues for men center around our swimmers. In most cases, the only test you'll need is your semen analysis, but it is possible you may undergo additional testing if the analysis suggests any problems. Let's take a look at what issues these tests might reveal.

- Low sperm quantity (oligospermia)

An average human male ejaculation contains about 180 million sperm, according to Dr. Charles Lindemann's lab at Oakland University. While your clinic may have its own criterion here, having fewer than 15 million sperm per milliliter or fewer than 40 million sperm total in a single ejaculate generally qualifies as a low sperm count, which in medical terms is called "oligospermia".

Now it might seem crazy that your sperm count could be considered low if you're producing 20 million sperm in a shot. While it only takes one sperm to fertilize an egg, very few sperm make it all the way to the fallopian tubes, and even fewer make it to the egg. Some estimates have found that even in a typical ejaculation of *hundreds of millions* of sperm, only a *couple hundred of them* may make it far enough to actually have a chance to fertilize the egg. Who knew sperm faced such tough odds?

Obviously, this causes a simple probability issue if the amount of sperm in your ejaculate is lower than typical, and some intervention may be needed to increase the likelihood of one of your sperm cells meeting your partner's egg.

- No sperm at all (azoospermia)

In rarer situations, your semen analysis may show that your ejaculate contains no sperm at all. Doctors call this condition "azoospermia." This can be a particularly emotionally devastating diagnosis, but it is not as uncommon as we might think: according to Johns Hopkins, azoospermia affects about 1% of all men, and 10% of men in couples with infertility.

If you receive this diagnosis, the most likely next step will be further testing to determine whether the azoospermia is caused by a lack of sperm production or a blockage somewhere along the way (see "plumbing issues" below). These tests will reveal possible courses of treatment. While this is a challenging diagnosis, we'll see later how advancements in reproductive assistance technology are making it possible in some cases for males with azoospermia to still have children that share their genetics.

- Poor sperm quality

The semen analysis also looks at the quality of your sperm, judged primarily by two factors: how well your sperm move (called "motility" in medical terms), and whether they have a normal shape (called their "morphology"). For motility, we want as many sperm as possible to be capable of forward movement—not swimming in a circle or wiggling around unable to advance. On the morphology size, we want sperm with a normal looking oval-shaped head and a long tail—it's relatively normal for many sperm to have deformations like small heads, long tails, or even having two heads or two tails. While what is considered "normal" varies by clinic, according to the Stony Brook University School of Medicine, labs generally look for at least 50% of sperm to have typical motility, and at least 30% to have typical morphology to be considered in the "normal" range.

This causes an issue for the same reasons of probability as having a low sperm count. If you have many sperm, but a higher percent are unable to move forward properly, or a high percent have deformations, there may not be enough "normal" sperm to make it to the egg and fertilize it. If your testing reveals sperm quality issues, you may want to look back at the list in chapter 1 of ways to potentially increase sperm quality over time.

- "Plumbing" issues

Finally, there may be blockages or other issues with the "plumbing" of your reproductive apparatus. In these cases, the doctor may wish to conduct further testing, such as ultrasounds or even a biopsy of your testicles. There are myriad potential issues here, from blockages in the testes, to blockages in the vas deferens or elsewhere in the reproductive tract.

This covers the most common issues your testing might reveal. If one of these diagnoses applies to you, you might be feeling upset, confused, angry, or all of the above. This is totally normal and expected. First, remember that much about these factors comes down to the random forces of biology, and the reasons for this diagnosis are largely out of your control. And remember you're not alone: according to the Cleveland Clinic, about half of infertility cases involve factors from the man.

Common Issues with the Female Reproductive Apparatus

Next, let's look at what testing may reveal about your partner. With more complex testing come more complex root causes, so the list of potential issues is longer.

- Irregular ovulation, or lack of ovulation

Blood work and ultrasounds could reveal issues with ovulation—the release of an egg which usually occurs about two weeks before a woman's period. The issue could simply be one of irregularity—your partner may only have a period once every several months, or your partner's periods may be totally unpredictable. The testing could also show that your partner is not actually ovulating—referred to as "anovulation." This is usually caused by hormonal imbalance. Anovulation can be marked by a total lack of a period, or your partner may still have menstrual flow but not release an egg. The problem here is pretty obvious: if no egg is released, there is no egg to be fertilized.

- Egg quality issues

Issues of egg quality are a bit harder to pin down than issues of sperm quality—it's easy to "extract" and examine sperm, but far more intrusive and impractical to extract a woman's eggs. Hence, doctors generally look at hormone levels from blood tests to assess whether there may be egg quality issues at play, and consider the whole spectrum of information about your partner's reproductive health in making this determination.

For instance, conditions like PCOS (see below) often go hand in hand with egg quality issues. Another example: if the level of follicle stimulating hormone ("FSH") is high, it basically indicates that your partner's body is working harder than usual to get the ovaries to produce and release eggs, which could indicate lower overall egg quality. Your doctor should explain their assessment of all relevant information. As always, don't be afraid to ask them to repeat or explain things in simpler language.

So why is this a problem? Just as with sperm quality issues, having egg quality issues decreases the chance of normal conception and formation of a normal, healthy embryo.

- Egg quantity issues

Just as with sperm, egg quantity varies from woman to woman. It's important to note that a woman is born with a set number of eggs (usually around a million), which diminishes naturally over time. Of course, a woman does not release one million eggs in her lifetime—there is attrition through ovulation, and because some eggs simply never fully develop and release.

When one's egg quantity is lower than typical, the probability of conception may be decreased. This is generally diagnosed based on assessment of all relevant health information for your partner. One hormone in particular, antimullerian hormone (or AMH), serves as a proxy for information about how many eggs are left in your partner's ovarian reserves. Based on AMH level and other information, your RE may conclude that your partner has a lower egg reserve, sometimes officially diagnosed as diminished ovarian reserve, or DOR.

- PCOS

Polycystic ovarian syndrome or PCOS is a hormonal imbalance that leads to development of cysts within, and enlargement of, the ovaries. PCOS is relatively common, affecting somewhere between 6-12% of women of reproductive age according to the CDC. It can cause painful, irregular, or heavy periods, acne, and many other symptoms including difficulty conceiving. While women with PCOS can get pregnant naturally, it is associated with an increased likelihood of infertility. This may be because PCOS can lead to other conditions described here, such as egg quality issues, irregular periods, and cysts.

- Endometriosis

Endometriosis is another relatively common condition, affecting somewhere between 2-10% of women of reproductive age per the Johns Hopkins School of Medicine. This happens when tissue which typically grows inside the uterus grows outside of it—for example in the fallopian tubes or on the ovaries. Endometriosis causes painful periods and pelvic discomfort. Similar to PCOS, having endometriosis does not necessarily prevent getting pregnant naturally, but does raise the likelihood of experiencing infertility. Endometriosis may make it more challenging to conceive because it can contribute to other conditions on this list such as egg quality and quantity issues.

- Anatomical issues—lesions, misshapen uterus, and blockages

Your partner may undergo investigation via ultrasound to look for any atypical structural issues with her reproductive system. A uterus is typically pear shaped, however, it is possible for women to have a uterus shaped in different ways, such as a heart shape. Other abnormalities may also be present, such as lacking one or both fallopian tubes. A second group of issues is related to lesions, polyps, scar tissue, and other features that can be present in the reproductive system.

Ultrasound investigation could also reveal blockages at various paths within your partner's reproductive system; for instance, there may be a blockage in one or both fallopian tubes. These anatomical issues, if present, can make it harder for egg and sperm to meet, or make it less likely for an embryo to successfully implant in the uterus.

- Implantation issues

In some cases there may be conditions that make it less likely for an embryo to implant in your partner's uterus. There could be multiple issues at play here—the uterine lining may not be as thick as it should be to promote the best chance of conception, or there could be other genetic or immunological factors at play that are making it more challenging for an embryo to successfully implant. Obviously if this is the case, it is far less likely for even a healthy, normal embryo to lead to ongoing pregnancy.

Implantation issues are typically diagnosed after you've already started fertility treatments, particularly if you attempt multiple IVF embryo transfers without getting pregnant.

OTHER COMMON ISSUES

Your clinic may also run a variety of blood tests which could reveal issues you, your partner, or both of you have that could cause difficulty conceiving. Broadly speaking, those issues fall into two categories: immunity, and genetics. Both categories are complex and can affect conceiving and growing a baby in myriad ways. Here are brief overviews of these types of issues.

- Immunological issues

Some conditions involving the immune/autoimmune system, such as Lupus or certain thyroid disorders, may play a role in creating and allowing healthy embryos to implant successfully in the uterus. While this is generally more pertinent to your partner, if either of you are aware that you have any immune or autoimmune issues, or if your blood work reveals such an issue, your doctor may incorporate treatments to address it as part of your overall plan.

- Genetic issues

It's possible to go through life with certain genetic markers that don't cause any issue for us, but which we could pass on to our kids. This can be the case even if you and your extended family are all healthy. Some of these genetic markers can lower the likelihood that you and your partner will produce healthy, genetically normal embryos. With some diseases such as Tay-Sachs, the doctors may review both of your genetic testing to see if one or both of you are carriers.

While having a genetic issue is relatively unlikely, it can make a difference in your treatment plan—we'll discuss genetic testing for embryos more later, but technology has made it possible to pre-test whether the embryos we form are genetically normal before we try to implant them—without damaging the embryo. If you and your partner have any genetic markers that could cause issues, using this genetic screening may increase your chances for success.

- Unexplained Infertility

Finally, after all that testing, it is possible there may be no obvious reason you're having difficulty conceiving. Indeed, per the Loma Linda Center for Fertility, somewhere between 15-30% of couples ultimately receive the (real and common) diagnosis of "unexplained infertility."

Receiving this diagnosis can be very frustrating. If you and your partner fall into the "unexplained infertility" category, know that it's perfectly justified to feel upset. It's easy to understand why: we live in an age where information about many complex subjects is instantaneously accessible. This makes it difficult to accept that there are some things we don't know, particularly involving the biological mechanisms at play to create a child.

The good news: if you have unexplained infertility, the suite of potential treatments is still available to you. At the very least, your RE will review all of you and your partner's test results and make a reasoned recommendation about the best next step. To help you prepare, we'll next look at some questions you can ask and bring with you to your appointment to ensure you fully understand the diagnosis and your test results.

NAVIGATING THE DIAGNOSIS APPOINTMENT: QUESTIONS TO ASK

As I mentioned, Olivia and I were surprised at how emotional and anxiety-provoking our appointment to review test results was. It's a major moment in your journey! Because of our experience in that appointment, we decided from then on we would always write down our questions before each appointment. We started a list a few days in advance, added questions here or there, then reviewed them on the drive to the clinic. This helped us make sure we had captured everything we wanted to know about, and prevented us from having to worry about remembering all the questions in the middle of a discussion. Here is a list of questions you can bring with you to the appointment to discuss your test results to help ensure you understand all of the information.

- In your opinion, what course of treatment gives us the best chance of success?
- Are there any lifestyle changes you'd recommend which could help optimize our chances for success?
- It sounds like you're recommending (fill in the particular treatment e.g., IVF or IUI). Could there be any benefit to attempting any lower level interventions first?
- How frequently do you treat couples who have a comparable situation to ours, and is there anything in your experience that is most helpful for couples similar to us?
- Are you satisfied we've got all the testing results necessary to make the best decision? Is there anything else we should be looking at or tests we should pursue before settling on a course of treatment?

- For each of our possible treatment options, what happens from here? What would the timeline and next steps look like?
- In addition to these questions, there are three general questions you should always feel empowered to ask and use:
- Can you repeat that/could you walk us through that information once more?
- Can you explain that in simpler terms?
- Can my partner and I confer for a minute to make sure we've covered all the information we need?

It can feel uncomfortable to ask for clarification, but go into the meeting with resolve to use this question anytime you or your partner feel any confusion. You may be reviewing a large volume of highly technical, scientific information. You may see an RE who, while highly qualified, is not skilled at explaining complex medical tests concisely. Likewise, it is entirely appropriate to ask for a minute to confer with your partner, take a breath, and review whether you have any additional questions.

Bring these questions to the meeting, and write down any others you have. You'll feel better prepared and more empowered to listen and absorb the information so you can decide what course of treatment is right.

~ ~ ~

I hugged Olivia while we waited for the financial counselor to return.

"I can't believe it," she said. "How did the regular OB not know my AMH was low? Here I figured we just had some unknown factor preventing us from getting pregnant, and now all of a sudden it's my eggs?"

"I know, I know. I was convinced we'd start on IUIs but IVF is so much more...so much more work, more time, more money...just more everything."

Olivia sighed. "Yeah, now I'm picturing having to get a boatload of shots everyday."

"Well, the doctor did say there was a chance with IUIs. We could at least try it. And who knows, it could work?"

"I don't know," she shook her head. "She said we have a 5-10% chance of success with IUI. I wouldn't call those great odds. What if we do three IUIs, they don't work, and then we end up six months from now even more desperate, back at square one, and with probably even fewer good eggs?"

"I know, love. I know..." I trailed off.

Olivia was silent for a few moments. She closed her eyes. Then she turned back to me. The mistiness in her eyes had turned to steeled resolve: "We've already lost out on over a year of trying. We have to do whatever it takes. If IVF gives us a 50/50 chance, that's the best we can get. Shots or no shots, we can't waste any more time. We have to do this. We just have to"

"Ok, love. Are you sure?"

She nodded.

"Are you positive?"

She nodded again.

"Then we're doing IVF."

The financial counselor knocked twice, waited a beat, and stepped back in. "I know you have a lot to think about, so take some time and just call when you're ready. I'm happy to answer any questions, navigate things with insurance, or help in any other way. Call or email me anytime."

"Actually," said Olivia, "We're ready. Let's start the paperwork for IVF. What do we need to do?"

~ ~ ~

WHAT HAPPENS NEXT?

The next step is for you and your partner to consider the information you've received from your doctor in combination with your finances and insurance, and to choose a course of treatment.

For us, the clarity of our diagnosis helped make our choice to proceed to IVF easier, even if it was sooner than we anticipated. We knew Olivia potentially had some degree of diminished ovarian reserve, and this made IVF by far the most likely road to success. We had also done our research in advance—just like you're doing now—to understand potential diagnoses and treatments.

To fill in the full picture, let's now look in detail at those potential treatments your RE may recommend.

Chapter 5

Potential Treatments

Visions of maple syrup stands, scenic leafy backroads, and quaint village squares lined with steepled white churches floated through my brain as I stuffed a sweater and pair of camp socks in my dark blue overnight bag. We were off to Vermont for a brief but necessary early fall respite before starting our first round of IVF. The next few months were sure to be busy, and a bit of foliage, a nice dinner, and some relaxing walks would be a welcome tonic before starting nightly shots and early morning trips to the clinic.

As I finished packing, I could hear Olivia downstairs on the phone speaking with the pharmacy. We'd learned that IVF drugs are considered specialty medicines, so procuring them was no simple matter of driving to the nearest Walgreens. Rather, we had to call a special pharmacy (after securing approval from our primary insurance, of course) and make arrangements for them to ship the drugs directly to our door.

With everything packed, I headed downstairs. As Olivia ran through our list of medicines, the necessary syringe parts, and disposal equipment that would be coming our way, I looked over our treatment calendar for what seemed like the hundredth time. Our IVF clinic was extremely thorough, and had walked us through exactly what drugs to administer at what time on which days over the weeks ahead.

It was a Friday afternoon. The following Monday, either in the morning or the evening (our choice, based on convenience for our schedules), we would fill the syringes and do the first injection. Each day thereafter, we'd administer the same drugs, potentially adjusting the amounts based on our RE's assessment of progress given every-other-day ultrasound checks. If all went well, we would go to the clinic ten to fourteen days later, and the RE would surgically remove as many eggs as possible with a goal of them fertilizing, growing, and ultimately…hopefully…

But I was getting ahead of myself. Many of the podcasts I'd listened to recommended taking fertility treatment one step at a time and remaining in the present moment. Good advice, but not always easy.

"Keegan!" Suddenly, Olivia called me into the other room. Her phone was in her left hand, the speaker covered with her right hand.

"There's a big problem," she continued. "The pharmacy doesn't do Sunday or Monday deliveries, and one of my meds has to be refrigerated as soon as it arrives. They do Saturday delivery and overnight, so they can come tomorrow, but we're leaving! The drugs would be ruined by the time we get back on Sunday if they sit outside!"

I felt a flash of anger. Couldn't even one solitary step on our journey be easy? Briefly, the smell of maple syrup evaporated as my turbulent mind jumped to the path of least resistance, simply canceling the trip.

Then I took a breath. "Ok, let's think. There has to be a way to make this work, and we need this rest time. So the meds have to come tomorrow, there's no other option. Can they ship them somewhere close to where we're staying?"

We put the pharmacy rep on speaker and found out this would indeed be possible. But then logistical questions crept up. Were we certain our Airbnb had a fridge? It was a shared kitchen—would we have to explain to another guest why we had huge boxes from a pharmacy taking up half the fridge? Not our idea of a relaxing time.

Then we looked for nearby UPS stores—we'd have to drive two hours roundtrip to a location in northern Massachusetts. By the time we went there and back, we'd have spent more of our vacation driving than relaxing.

"Ok, so I guess that won't work either," Olivia stated dejectedly. What other options do we have?"

"Well…" I wracked my brain. There had to be something we could do.

"Wait!" Synapses fired at long last. "What about someone coming and putting the meds in our fridge? A friend, a neighbor…someone? We could leave a key, explain what's happening, and just have the meds delivered here tomorrow."

It was unstated, but we both knew the hurdle here: apart from our immediate family, no one else knew we were doing IVF, and none of our family members were close enough to manage the pickup. No one else knew we'd been struggling to conceive, and we couldn't ask someone to come and put a box of drugs in our fridge without explaining what was going on.

"Hm, that could just work," pondered Olivia. "I guess we could tell…the Millers? I'd be comfortable telling them what happened. Remember, it took them a long time to have their son and it was a hard pregnancy—I think they'd understand."

Two minutes later, we had the pharmacy rep on hold while we called up our friends. Another two minutes later, we were finalizing the details and the pharmacy rep was giving us tracking numbers.

"We made it work!" she exclaimed. "Now—go hide a set of keys somewhere safe. I'll whip up a batch of brownies to leave to thank the Millers."

We set off on our tasks. I was content to have the issue with the drugs sorted, but felt a lingering sense of anger that yet another step in this difficult journey had to be even harder than necessary. I headed out to set up the keys, comforted that at least I would still get some maple syrup in the days ahead.

~ ~ ~

Olivia and I look back on this story now and laugh, but it certainly wasn't amusing at the time. The fact is, going through fertility treatments involves a lot of logistics, particularly if you're doing IVF. It's probably been a long road just to get to the point of doing treatments, so the difficulties of managing the plans—let alone shots—can be a challenge in and of itself, as we learned on that autumnal day.

Despite the difficulties, getting to the point of developing a treatment plan can feel very positive. Having an idea of what is preventing you from conceiving might provide some small sense of regaining control. Your RE should have given you their assessment of what's going on at your appointment to review test results, and should have offered an idea of what treatments might be suitable.

Your doctor may suggest a very clear direction—for instance, going straight to IVF if that's what fits your situation. Alternatively, your doctor may offer two or three possible courses of treatment, give their best advice, and allow you and your partner to decide or give input as to what course you prefer. Regardless of which approach your doctor takes, make sure you have all necessary information and sufficient time to think it over with your partner and make a reasoned choice.

You may also be constrained by requirements of insurance or finances. Our insurance required us to try three rounds of less intrusive interventions before proceeding to IUI or IVF. Thankfully we'd already met this requirement through Olivia's OB prescribing letrozole, but this is why it's wise to review insurance information (if you have coverage) before getting started. We could easily have found ourselves frustrated and blindsided by having to revert to three months of lower-level interventions in order to qualify for our IVF benefits. If you're paying out of pocket, you'll consider your budget and choose the option that works best.

That all said, it's time to delve into the potential treatments you and your partner may undergo. As with the last chapter on diagnoses, this is not intended to be an exhaustive list of all possible treatments—indeed, podcasts, websites, and other specialized books cover these in greater detail (and are more qualified to do so). However, I want to outline the basics of possible treatments, what they're meant to help overcome, how they work, and some benefits and challenges each one may present.

POSSIBLE TREATMENTS FOR LOW/NO SPERM

If you have low or no sperm, treatments are available which could allow you to still have children biologically. These generally involve surgically extracting sperm from your testes. While your semen analysis may have found few or no sperm present, it may be possible for a doctor to find sperm cells via biopsy. And it only takes one normal sperm cell to make an embryo!

Note that if you have to undergo a biopsy to extract sperm cells, your partner must also undergo IVF egg retrieval. This is because of the long journey a sperm takes to meet the egg described earlier—if the doctor is able to extract, say, five, or two, or perhaps one single normal sperm cell from your testes, it would be a waste to place those sperm in your partner; so few sperm would have almost no chance of fertilizing an egg released naturally. While it is a burden for your partner to undergo IVF egg extraction, it is necessary in this case to give you a shot at success.

If you undergo this type of treatment, your IVF lab will almost certainly also use a procedure called intracytoplasmic sperm injection, or "ICSI" (pronounced ICK-see), to further improve your odds. In this procedure, an embryologist in the IVF lab uses a very small pipette to "pick up" a single sperm cell and inject it directly in one of your partner's eggs. How amazing is that? It takes all the probability out of having egg and sperm meet and gets them directly together. Of course, this doesn't necessarily mean the egg and sperm will combine to make a healthy, high-quality embryo that implants and grows, and so forth—but this opens up the possibility of success that otherwise might have been impossible.

A quick side note: ICSI is not just for couples where the man has a low sperm count. ICSI is relatively common, and may be helpful if you have a normal quantity of sperm but low motility, or if you and your partner go through an IVF round and have a very low number of embryos fertilized. Thus, many couples undergoing IVF use ICSI regardless of sperm count.

Letrozole/Clomid: Boosting Ovulation

One minimally invasive treatment option is for your partner to take medications like letrozole or clomid. These drugs work to regulate hormones and stimulate ovulation. This increases the chance of your partner releasing an egg so you can have sex at the optimal time. These drugs can be useful in several situations.

First, if your partner is not ovulating or has irregular ovulation, these drugs can help make ovulation predictable. You can then have timed intercourse and increase the likelihood of sperm and egg meeting. This method is most likely to work if there are no other significant issues.

Second, these drugs are sometimes used in combination with other treatments like IUI in order to boost chances of success. Again here, it's all about timing. Ensuring and stimulating ovulation raises the chance for conception.

While these can be effective options, these drugs act powerfully on your partner's hormones and can cause very unpleasant side effects including mood swings, nausea, abdominal discomfort, and more. These side effects can in some cases be severe. While Olivia didn't have any particularly nasty side effects from letrozole, many women in the infertility community refer to these drugs with nicknames like "the Devil," which indicates just how unpleasant they can be. Remember this will not be true for every woman—some tolerate them with few side effects. However, knowledge is power. Be extra patient if your partner is prescribed these drugs, and plan in advance to do some nice things (like those discussed earlier!) to help her make it through the time when she is taking them.

IUI: THE TURKEY BASTER

Now, we get to the first of the "big guns" of infertility treatment: intrauterine insemination, or IUI. This procedure is usually performed by a doctor, but can also be performed by nurses (who, rest assured, are also highly trained). It is, in essence, exactly what it sounds like: the medical professional takes semen and injects it directly in your partner's uterus. More semen in the uterus (ideally) means more sperm in the fallopian tubes and greater chances of conception.

For an IUI, your doctor may recommend supplemental treatments to help increase your odds of success. First, your partner may take ovulation-stimulating medicine like clomid or letrozole as part of the preparation process to encourage ovulation and (possibly) increase the number of eggs released. Second, your partner may also take what is called a "trigger shot"—a shot of hormones that induces ovulation—about 24-36 hours before the IUI to ensure the timing of ovulation is optimized to when your semen is introduced. Finally, your semen is specially prepared for the IUI—

they are washed and concentrated in the lab to ensure as many as possible end up in the uterus.

The procedure itself is surprisingly quick, often just a few minutes from start to finish. In many cases, it does not even require an operating room. Your partner generally remains fully alert with no anesthesia required. The doctor or nurse brings in the specially prepared vial of your semen, inserts a tube up and through the cervix into your partner's uterus, and then pops the sperm in. Your partner may experience some minor discomfort during the actual insertion process.

Collectively, IUIs have an average of anywhere from a 5-25% success rate depending on you and your partner's health, age, and the root cause of your infertility, according to the Pacific Fertility Center of Los Angeles. Thus, it can be a great lower-cost and lower-intensity option for couples whose testing suggests there is a good chance for conception through this route. That said, recent research has found that for couples trying IUI, those who find success usually do so within the first 3-4 tries. Thus, if IUI does not lead to pregnancy within 3-4 tries, it may mean IVF or other more intensive intervention is necessary to increase your chances for conception.

So what's your role in IUI? Your biggest job is to support your partner and take steps to boost your own mental and physical wellness. Your only specific "contribution" is providing the semen sample. Whether you're allowed to be present for the actual procedure depends on your clinic's rules and procedures. If you can be there, I strongly suggest you go; it's an important bonding moment for you and your partner. Even if you can't go into the procedure room, go along for the drive and to be a supporting presence. After all, you'll probably need to be there to provide the semen anyway!

If for some reason you can't be present on the day of the procedure, you may need to provide semen in advance, which the lab will freeze and thaw for use (note that freezing can cause some slight degradation in sperm number and quality; usually this is not a significant issue, however, this option may not be available if you have a lower sperm count).

IVF

Now we come to the big one—in vitro fertilization, or IVF. While you may have heard people colloquially refer to IVF as "the test tube baby" procedure, the image this elicits of a mad scientist pouring the contents of one tube into another is far from reality. Put very simply, IVF is a process of growing and extracting eggs from your partner, mixing them with your sperm in a lab setting, allowing any resulting embryos to grow for 3-6 days, then putting one or more of the embryos back in your partner's uterus in hopes of conception. IVF can significantly increase your chances of pregnancy because it circumvents many potential issues: it extracts eggs, mixes them with sperm to encourage fertilization, and delivers an embryo directly to the uterus at the proper time to maximize the chance of implantation.

However, IVF is not a silver bullet. On average, the success rate of a live healthy birth for each cycle is somewhere in the 25-45% range according to the CDC fertility website depending on your particular health situation. Over the course of three cycles of IVF, the cumulative success rate for a live birth reaches around 45-53%, according to the National Institute for Health and Care Excellence out of the UK.

While technology continues to improve, doing IVF is not a perfect guarantee. I'll admit this came as a surprise to me the more we learned about IVF; my impression was that it somehow just worked. Though I wish it provided more of a guarantee, knowing the overall odds helped me adjust my expectations.

Now, let's examine what actually occurs during IVF. An entire "cycle" of IVF from preparation through to embryo transfer can take anywhere from 4-8 weeks. Below, I break the cycle down step by step, looking at what you are doing and what your partner is doing at each step

- Step One: Preparation/Cycle Alignment (1-3 weeks)
    - *What's your partner doing?* Preparing for the IVF cycle, which may involve taking certain hormones as prescribed by the RE and/or taking birth control if it's necessary to align her cycle with the clinic's schedule, a practice called "batch" scheduling in which a group of women at a clinic all undergo a cycle simultaneously. So for instance, you and 15 other couples may prepare and go through a cycle with a shared target window for egg retrievals. Other clinics don't follow batch scheduling and simply work based on each woman's cycle. Batch cycling with birth control does not have any effect on chances of success.
    - *What are you doing?* Taking care of yourself, supporting your partner, and potentially doing your homework and research on how to give shots in preparation for step two!
- Step Two: Growing the Eggs (a/k/a Shot Time) (1-2 weeks)
    - *What's your partner doing?* Taking one or more injections of fertility medications per day to stimulate her ovaries to grow as many follicles (sacs containing eggs) as possible. She is also going to the fertility clinic roughly every other day for monitoring appointments, during which she'll undergo an ultrasound and blood work. Based on the results of those tests, the doctor may adjust doses for the fertility medications. The doctor is managing a delicate dance: you want as many follicles as possible, but they grow at different rates. Thus, you want smaller ones to

grow without causing others to become too large, which can result in eggs that are not usable. By the end of this, she will likely be very uncomfortable because the drugs are forcing her ovaries to grow far more eggs than they typically would; as a result, they are becoming swollen.

  - *What are you doing?* At the very least, you're taking care of yourself and supporting your partner—try to cook or pick up some favorite foods during this time to make both of your lives easier. If you're really working to earn your merit badges, you may be the one giving the shots! If this is the case, watch instructional videos from the clinic carefully before beginning—it can be intimidating and anxiety-provoking at first (see the next chapter for more on giving shots and how to prepare). Be mindful of how she's feeling physically during these weeks and be ready to help her out. Avoid planning any rigorous travel or activities in the final days leading up to the egg retrieval.

- Step Three: The Trigger Shot (After roughly 1-2 weeks of IVF meds, based on when your clinic tells you)
  - *What's your partner doing?* At this point, the RE believes you've maximized the number of growing follicles. Your clinic then reaches out with a specific time at which your partner must take what is called the "trigger shot," which is different medicine from the IVF drugs. The trigger shot tells her ovaries it is time to ovulate in 24-36 hours. This ensures the timing of the egg retrieval surgery aligns with ovulation so it is as easy as possible for the doctor to extract eggs. The clinic provides a precise time at which you must administer the trigger shot; it's critical to

follow this instruction exactly and do the shot at the prescribed time.

  - *What are you doing?* You may be administering the trigger shot—or at least helping to ensure the timing is precise. I can't underscore this enough—if the clinic says you need to administer the shot at 10:30 pm on Tuesday, ensure you do it at that exact time.

- Step Four: Egg Retrieval (1 day—procedure usually lasts anywhere up to an hour)
  - *What is your partner doing?* Undergoing the procedure to remove as many eggs as possible. Your partner will be under anesthesia for the surgery itself, which lasts anywhere from 30-60 minutes. The doctor or clinic should let you know how many eggs they extracted after the surgery. Expect to be at the clinic for a total of anywhere from 3-4 hours including preparation time and time for your partner to come back around from anesthesia.
  - *What are you doing?* Making time to be at the clinic; not only will your partner be under anesthesia and need a driver, this is a big day for both of you. She's undergone a physically taxing process, and both of you will be feeling hopeful but nervous. Take time off if you can. It's also likely you'll provide a semen sample on this day for combining with your partner's eggs.
- Step Five: Mix Sperm and Eggs (same day as egg retrieval)
  - *What is your partner doing?* Relaxing on the couch at home post-egg retrieval.

    - *What are you doing?* Also relaxing on the couch at home post-egg retrieval! Give yourselves a rest. Meanwhile, back at the lab, your sperm and your partner's eggs will be mixed together to mingle (or combined via ICSI).

- Step Six: Fertilization and Growth (takes place generally over 4-6 days)
    - *What are you and your partner doing?* At this point, you're both just waiting. Your partner may start other meds to prepare her body for the transfer during this period. Over the five or so days following egg retrieval, the clinic will be in regular touch about progress. The reason for the wait is to allow the embryos to develop; this allows the clinic's lab to assess their growth and choose ones which appear to be growing normally, and that as such give the best shot for implantation. You can expect them to call within about 24 hours of egg retrieval to let you know how many eggs were fertilized. Then, they will update you every day or two thereafter as to how the eggs are growing. In nearly all cases, the number of eggs and embryos will decrease over time—if you get 10 eggs for example, it's common to end up with anywhere from 2-5 viable embryos at the end of the growth period. This period is quite nerve-wracking, and given the natural attrition, is often called "the IVF Hunger Games"—a reference to a dystopian book series where people are forced into a battle royale competition in which only one survives— by couples in the infertility community. I cover this period in much greater depth in the next chapter.

- Step Seven: Transferring Embryos Back to Uterus (usually 4-6 days post egg retrieval)
    - *What is your partner doing?* Your partner goes into the clinic and has one or more embryos transferred into her uterus. Then, 10-14 days after the transfer, she goes to the clinic for an hCG pregnancy test via blood work (as opposed to home urine pregnancy tests, which are less accurate).
    - *What are you doing?* Going to the clinic on transfer day for moral support! Some clinics may allow partners in the actual procedure room for the transfer, while others do not. If you can attend, you should do so. Even if you can't be in the procedure room, you should go for moral support. Beyond this, you'll be crossing your fingers and planning fun activities to keep you and your partner's minds off the "two week wait" as much as possible.
    - *A word on fresh vs. frozen embryo transfers:* The description to this point covers a "fresh" embryo transfer—one in which the transfer takes place immediately after the embryos grow following an IVF cycle. It is also possible to freeze embryos to either "bank" extras for later use, or to conduct genetic testing, and then thaw and implant the frozen embryos later. If doing a frozen embryo transfer, the entire process is less labor intensive—your partner generally prepares by taking some hormones and medications for the 2-4 weeks leading up to the embryo transfer, and conducts a few monitoring appointments to ensure her uterine lining has thickened to give the best shot at implantation.

On transfer day, the embryologist thaws and prepares the embryo, and the doctor places it in your partner's uterus.

- *A word on single vs multiple embryo transfers:* These days, it is most common to only transfer one embryo at a time, often called an "elective single embryo transfer," or "ESET." In the earlier days of IVF, the standard course was to implant multiple embryos in order to provide the best chances for conception. This is why you may remember hearing many stories about IVF multiple pregnancies (twins, triplets, etc.) in years past. Times have changed. Now, in most cases, clinics recommend transferring one healthy embryo at a time as the best course of action. You might be thinking—why wouldn't we want to potentially save time and money and just transfer three or four good embryos at once? The answer is that multiple gestation pregnancies of twins, triplets, or more are considered "high-risk", as they carry increased odds of miscarriage, pre-term birth, and other complications. We are also fortunate to live in times where technology has improved, so between the IVF lab and genetic testing (if you opt to test your embryos), clinics are getting increasingly skilled at identifying which embryos are most likely to lead to a healthy baby. I imagined doing IVF meant a greater chance for twins or triplets, and a few people we told we were doing IVF made friendly but ill-informed jibes about ending up as "octo-mom." Listen to what your doctor has to say, and remember that having one healthy baby at a time gives you and your partner the best chance at a healthy and normal pregnancy.

And that's the IVF overview! The last step is of course the infamous two week wait—which is in some ways the most challenging. A final note: the outline above is the *ideal* progression of steps—but as with so much in infertility, things may not always go to plan. The list below explains what could happen at each step, and what that means for your treatment cycle. I share these not to provoke anxiety, but rather to provide full information so you're prepared. These are only intended to describe what *may* happen—in the next chapter, I discuss how you can be prepared to manage your and your partner's feelings for various challenges like these.

- *Canceled cycle*: If your partner's ovaries do not respond well to the IVF meds (i.e., they're not growing many follicles/eggs), it's possible the doctor may recommend canceling the cycle. This is hard to hear, but the doctor wants to avoid performing an invasive surgery which may not yield many (or any) eggs. One possibility here is converting the cycle to an IUI instead; this can make it feel like the effort and discomfort have been worthwhile and provides at least a chance for conception.
- *No eggs fertilize*: Sadly, it's possible you may combine eggs and sperm and not have any eggs fertilize—particularly if the egg retrieval does not yield many eggs to begin with. Your doctor should schedule a follow up to discuss what occurred, what may have caused it, and what they might do differently if you try another cycle.
- *No embryos viable for implantation*: It's possible to have some number of embryos fertilized, but after 4-5 days, none of them survive.

Alternatively, the embryos may survive but the embryologist may find they are not good enough quality to be worth implanting. Again, your doctor should schedule a follow up to debrief what happened.

THE MOMENT OF TRUTH: THE PREGNANCY TEST AND "BETA DAY"

If you're doing IUI or IVF, your partner will probably have a blood draw pregnancy test scheduled for 10-14 days after the IUI or embryo transfer. The blood draw looks for the presence and level of human chorionic gonadotropin (hCG) in your partner's blood, as hCG is released and the level rises quickly after an embryo successfully implants in the uterus. This blood draw is often called a "beta," and many couples undergoing treatment call the day of the blood test "beta day." Needless to say, it's a big day.

But wait, you may think—I can run down to the pharmacy and get a pregnancy test in ten minutes, so why wait for a blood test at the clinic? It's true that home pregnancy tests, which use urine instead of blood, also detect the presence of hCG, but there is a key difference. A blood draw beta gives the exact level of hCG (measured in milli-international units per milliliter, or mIU/mL), whereas a positive home pregnancy test only indicates the amount of hCG exceeds a certain amount.

So why is this important? Well, some home pregnancy tests display a positive result when the amount of hCG is still quite low, particularly "early detection" tests, which are designed to pick up even very low levels of hCG in the earliest days of a pregnancy. The issue here is, the extremely early days of pregnancy are a delicate time. It's not uncommon for embryos to implant but for various (often genetic) reasons, fail in these very early days. When that happens, the woman would have what would seem like a slightly late period, but is in fact the (very early) end of that pregnancy. This is technically a miscarriage, often referred to as a "chemical pregnancy" because it is so early in the pregnancy that no significant symptoms or indications of pregnancy have really started.

So what does this have to do with the blood draw? The advantage of the beta (blood draw) hCG test is that it provides an exact hCG level. In early pregnancy, the level of hCG rises very quickly, generally doubling every 36-48 hours. Thus, the clinic will likely have your partner do at least two betas: one to confirm whether she is indeed pregnant, and a second to determine whether the hCG is going up at a proper rate. Simply taking home pregnancy tests can't reveal that level of specificity. Suffice to say, these betas are stressful, but important to ensure the clinic is managing your partner's health properly. We'll discuss betas further later on, including strategies to make it through what can be an anxiety-provoking time.

Treatments for Implantation Issues

Some couples who do IVF find they can create apparently normal embryos, but those embryos repeatedly fail to implant (in other words, the doctor transfers the embryo into your partner's uterus, but it does not result in a pregnancy). There are many potential root causes for this, and it can be a very challenging issue. Here are a few specialized procedures that your doctor may suggest if this occurs.

- *Assisted hatching*: Did you know human embryos have to "hatch"? It's sort of like a chicken from an egg, albeit at a much smaller scale. Doctors have found that some couples make embryos that have difficulty hatching, which can lower the likelihood of implantation and pregnancy. Assisted hatching is a laboratory procedure wherein the embryologist thins or makes a minor puncture to help your embryo hatch, thereby giving it a greater likelihood of implanting successfully.

- *Medication to thicken uterine lining:* To prepare for implantation and pregnancy, the uterus should develop a thick, hospitable lining for the embryo. Your doctor may find your partner's uterine lining is not thick enough to maximize chances for implantation. If this is the case, the doctor may prescribe hormones like estrogen, or other medicines, to help thicken the uterine lining.
- *Endometrial Receptivity Analysis (ERA) Test:* Another method that can help with implantation issues is the ERA test, sometimes referred to as the "ERA scratch" test. In this test, the RE biopsies (or removes) a small amount of the uterine lining. A laboratory then performs some sophisticated genetic testing on the lining sample. This testing allows the doctor to know when your partner's uterus is most receptive to implantation, as there can be variations from one woman to another. Improving the precision of timing can increase the chances of implantation and pregnancy.

PREIMPLANTATION GENETIC TESTING

Another major emerging treatment in the fertility world is preimplantation genetic testing (PGT), sometimes also called preimplantation genetic diagnosis (PGD) or preimplantation genetic screening (PGS). This procedure allows you to determine in advance whether embryos from an IVF cycle are genetically normal. This is important because even young, healthy couples produce some percent of embryos with genetic abnormalities. As age increases, particularly for the woman, the percentage of embryos with genetic abnormalities also increases. Thus, PGT allows you to select and transfer genetically normal embryos to increase the likelihood of successful implantation and a normal, healthy pregnancy.

How does this work? The embryologist biopsies (scrapes off) a tiny clump of cells from each embryo when it is about 5 days old. Then, the lab freezes the embryos and tests the clump of cells for genetic abnormalities. Within the next several weeks, results come back and your doctor tells you which embryos are genetically normal, and which are not.

Conducting PGT does not decrease the odds of implantation and pregnancy, even with the need to biopsy the embryo. Indeed, some studies suggest using PGT can significantly increase the odds of IVF success. If your partner is over 35, or if you have a history of embryo transfers that do not implant or result in miscarriages, this can be extremely helpful. Your doctor may also recommend PGT in advance if you and your partner have known markers based on your pre-IVF testing that could make it more likely for you to produce embryos with genetic issues.

An important note: fertility benefits almost never include PGT coverage, so basically everyone reading this can expect to have to pay out of pocket if you opt for PGT. While it is becoming more affordable as more labs offer this service, PGT generally costs anywhere from $1,500-$10,000 or more (as of 2022) depending on how many embryos you are sending for testing.

Your doctor should discuss PGT with you if they feel it is an option worth considering. As always, feel comfortable and empowered to ask questions like "What specifically about our situation makes you recommend considering PGT?" and, "In your estimation, how much might PGT increase our chances for success?"

This can be a huge help for couples in certain situations, so get the information you need, and you'll ultimately make the choice that's right for you.

SUPPLEMENTAL WELLNESS TREATMENTS

Everything listed above falls into a category we might call "health-based medicine," which is to say they're interventions designed to treat a specific diagnosed issue with you and your partner's health. A different approach is what you might call "wellness-based medicine." The difference is that wellness-based medicine focuses on things you can do everyday to maintain a high level of wellness. It's important to note that these are complementary, not contradictory, approaches—in other words, they may work most effectively together.

Here's an example of how these two approaches might work in tandem: if you're diagnosed with high cholesterol or blood pressure, a "health-based" approach would be if your doctor recommended taking a drug to decrease your levels. A "wellness-based" approach would be to start exercising and meditating daily to increase physical fitness and lower stress. In all likelihood, your doctor may recommend doing all of these actions to both address your immediate need via the medicine while also improving overall health habits.

Of course, the "right" approach here also depends on the situation. If you have a broken leg or have a heart attack, your immediate need is a health-based treatment in a hospital to address the very urgent issue. If on the other hand you, say, have slightly elevated blood pressure, your doctor may discuss wellness-interventions like an exercise program rather than prescribing medicine.

So what does this have to do with fertility? Well as you've likely seen, there are many complementary "wellness" treatments which some people opt to use while undergoing IVF, IUI, or other fertility treatments. Some of the most common include acupuncture and yoga (for your partner of course, but you can always do them too if you're into it!). Many fertility clinics even have in-house practitioners to provide yoga classes or acupuncture specifically designed to support fertility.

These can be great options. While the research on how acupuncture or yoga helps is mixed, I put things like yoga and acupuncture in the "it can't possibly hurt" category. If your partner likes doing them and they make her feel good, then by all means consider it if your doctor believes it is a good idea.

Making Sense of Wellness Treatments

For most people, considering wellness treatments won't be anything too controversial—your partner may opt to go to a couple sessions of acupuncture, or join a yoga class, or start eating more vegetables (any of which you can and should join in on!)

With that all said, there is also a massive apparatus on the internet proposing all sorts of suggestions for people experiencing infertility that I'd put in the category of "wellness" treatments. As with any information on the internet, be a cautious consumer. Many of the people spreading and sharing suggestions about certain vitamins, or supplements, or dietary changes, or types of exercises (and so on and so on) are not trained medical professionals. If it seems too good to be true, it probably is. The bottom line here, which should be no surprise, is: neither you nor your partner should do or take anything as a supplement to your fertility treatment that you haven't discussed with your doctor and received his or her approval.

Olivia went pretty frequently to both yoga and acupuncture during all of our IVF cycles. She also did acupuncture immediately before and after each embryo transfer. Did any of this make a difference as to the results of our treatment? We'll never know for sure, but it made her feel good mentally and physically. We were also fortunate: our fertility clinic had several acupuncturists who provided services in-house, and our local gym had a great weekly yoga class (which I even joined in on at times).

So as you consider what type of wellness treatments you or your partner are interested in, just remember to discuss anything with your doctor first, and be very cautious about any information that isn't from a trained medical professional. The internet is a great communication tool, but remember what our parents told us about jumping off a bridge—just because some person in Hawaii claims they ate nothing but canned pumpkin and an expensive supplement for two months before IVF and then had a baby doesn't make it a good or safe idea.

TO THE NEXT FRONTIER

As of 2022, the first baby born through IVF is just over forty years old. In the grand scheme of things, fertility treatments are an extremely young field of medicine. Yet in those forty years, the science and treatments have improved at warp speed.

Consider this small example: when IVF first came about, it was not possible to freeze embryos. General practice was to transfer several fresh embryos that resulted from an IVF cycle to maximize chances that one would implant and lead to a healthy birth. Eventually, embryo freezing advanced and became a more common practice. This was a game changer. Couples could now "bank" embryos they created and use them later. In some cases this could mean that instead of having to do three or more cycles of IVF to have several kids, a couple might only have to do one cycle, "bank" and freeze embryos (if they're lucky enough to have several normal ones), and potentially implant and have several babies from that single egg retrieval cycle.

But the freezing and thawing process was still imperfect—earlier in the 2000s, it was common for only 50% of embryos to survive the thawing process.

Then technology lept ahead again: by the early 2010s, embryo freezing had improved to the point where a good IVF lab could expect over 95% of embryos to survive thawing. Today, with a high quality clinic and lab, couples rarely need to worry about losing embryos in the thawing process. This is amazing progress; we can only imagine how advanced fertility treatment will become in the next forty years!

Now that we've covered the most common treatments, let's again step back and think about what might be going on with you and your partner. Starting treatments brings entirely new challenges and emotions, so the next chapter will help you understand what to expect.

CHAPTER 6

NAVIGATING THE UPS AND DOWNS OF TREATMENT

Covered from one end to the other in vials, tubes, syringes, needles, bottles of rubbing alcohol, and sterile pads, our bathroom counter looked more like an operating room tray than the spot where we brush our teeth.

The big moment was here; it was time to take out our IVF drugs, dose them into proper shots, and inject them into Olivia's abdomen, where hopefully they'd signal her ovaries to start working overtime. We'd spent the past week in full preparation mode. We read article after article, viewed what seemed like dozens of YouTube videos demonstrating IVF injections, and completed a "how to administer IVF medicines" online course from our clinic.

It was just after 7:45, and we'd decided 8:00 each evening would be our consistent shot time. The final countdown was on. After setting the materials up in the bathroom, I'd gone downstairs to our kitchen island, running through the how to course for a last refresher. I went through the checklist in my head: Get all medications out. Wipe down every surface, vial, and anything we touch with an alcohol wipe. Wash hands well with antibacterial soap before starting. Fill and mix meds if necessary. For pre-filled injectables, ensure I select the correct dosage amount. Triple check that everything is ready. "Pinch an inch" on Olivia's abdomen with my left hand, pick up the syringe in my right hand, and stick the needle swiftly and confidently in the apex of the tissue at a 90 degree angle. Release the abdominal tissue. Inject slowly. Remove the needle carefully. Place sterile gauze on the injection site. Repeat with other medicines, and finish with a bandage.

It was so bizarre. I'm not a medical professional, yet here I was feeling like a nurse welcoming a patient for a round of shots, and the patient just happened to be my wife!

"Ok," I croaked. "I think I might need to watch the step-by-step YouTube video from that nurse and follow along just to be sure."

Olivia drew a sharp inhale. "Alright. You're sure you understand all the steps?"

For an endless few seconds, I looked around and pondered. Was I sure? We had thousands of dollars worth of medicine stashed in our fridge and cabinets. Thankfully, our friends the Millers went above and beyond and stopped by while we enjoyed our weekend in Vermont to bring our large shipment of drugs inside and put them in the fridge. What if I messed up the dose after all that? If I gave too much, would Olivia's ovaries just blow up in awful discomfort? What if I spilled a vial on the floor? Would we have enough left? Would we have to rush order extra and pay sticker price?

I remembered the YouTube video and shook myself back to reality. We'd prepared. We'd overprepared.

"Yes. Sorry. Yes. I'm ready."

We went upstairs to the bathroom and I watched the nurse's YouTube video, following along and pausing as needed to catch up and complete each step. After five minutes of swabbing, removing caps from vials, mixing with sterile water, double checking doses, assembling syringes, and obsessively washing my hands several times more than necessary, everything was set.

I turned to Olivia. "Ready?"

Again, she drew in a rapid breath. "Hold on. Hold on." She put both hands on the bathroom counter, moved her feet backwards, and lowered her head between her elbows, drawing deep breaths.

"I just need to get myself ready," she said. "Maybe we need some music—something happy. Something to keep my mind occupied."

For the first of what would eventually be many times, I grabbed Olivia's phone and readied a soundtrack to accompany nightly shots.

"What are you in the mood for?" I asked.

"Hm…something peppy for sure…like Motown maybe?"

"Sure, upbeat…that works!" I responded.

YouTube came to the rescue, quickly directing me to The Supremes Greatest Hits. As the intro beat lilted forth, the room felt lighter. I waited, wanting to ensure she felt in control.

A slight smile spread across her face as the first chorus played.

"Ok. I'm ready."

I picked up the Follistim, which was the first drug on the list. I checked one last time to ensure I had the right dose, as Olivia sterilized a spot on her abdomen with rubbing alcohol. I pinched the inch with my left hand and picked up the syringe in my right, mentally calculating the angle and velocity to insert the needle as smoothly as possible—not so quick as to jab, but not so slow as to draw out the stabbing pain.

As Diana Ross sang in the background, I checked one last time. "You good?"

She nodded. I drew back the needle, breathed deeply…and thrust it forward.

~ ~ ~

In this chapter, we'll step away from the physical process of fertility treatment and focus on the mental toll. And make no mistake, there will be stressful times.

After all, starting fertility treatment elicits a strange mix of feelings. On one hand, it's exhilarating: this could really be it! After months or years of trying without success, this could actually lead to pregnancy and a baby. On the other hand, it's terrifying. The "what-ifs" start to run through your mind as you deal with the daily grind of treatment, consider what happens if this treatment or cycle doesn't work, and navigate the hardest part of all: the waiting.

That's right, after all the waiting you've endured already, a large part of fertility treatment involves—you guessed it—even more waiting! You may have to wait for insurance to approve a treatment cycle, or wait to align your partner's cycle in order to start a cycle, wait for daily results from ultrasounds to know how your partner's eggs are growing, or wait to know how many eggs were fertilized after an egg retrieval. And then there's the ultimate wait: the two week wait, with minutes seeming like hours as you obsess and count down to the day when you find out if your partner is pregnant.

So let's dig in. To be clear, this chapter addresses the timeframe from when you and your partner start treatment up to the point of getting the results of a pregnancy test to determine if those treatments worked. We'll look at what comes after the pregnancy test later.

REVERSED ROLES: MEN, WOMEN, AND WHAT IT MEANS TO BE STRONG

A quick thought experiment: what comes to mind when you envision a man who is strong? The first thing that probably flashes into your mind is a physically strong, emotionally stable, "manly" man, perhaps with requisite rippling biceps. You might then stop and consider that there are other things which make a person strong, but still—the initial image is deeply ingrained for most of us.

This brings us to the great irony of fertility treatments: in most cases, undergoing fertility treatment does not require any physical strength from the man. In fact, it's the woman who must literally be strong; her body endures the brunt of the journey and its hardships. For men, the fertility treatment journey calls on us to play the role of emotional supporter, a role more stereotypically expected of women. In this way, fertility treatment flips traditional roles on their head.

Unfortunately, we're often told that any reversal of these roles is something to be ashamed of. This can be a hard reality for us to fathom. Spending months or years in a role that is primarily focused on emotional support is precisely the kind of journey that society has least prepared us for. So if it feels challenging, we shouldn't be surprised!

My primary advice as we start is to be patient with yourself. As best as you can, try to view this as an opportunity to understand your own emotions better. This is a tremendous investment that can pay amazing dividends for your quality of life, especially as you look toward fatherhood. There is all sorts of research out there about how valuable it is to children to have fathers who are emotionally supportive and open. So while the fertility treatment journey isn't easy, it can actually set you up to be and feel like a more successful father!

It's also an opportunity to appreciate how physically strong and resilient your partner is. When I look back at our years of IVF, I am constantly in awe of what Olivia went through—hundreds of shots, multiple surgeries—and the grace and resilience with which she endured it—to say nothing of the intense pain and exertion of pregnancy and birth! It isn't easy to see your partner uncomfortable, but the physical tenacity fertility treatment requires of women can also help us shift our thinking.

With this frame, let's talk about some things you may be feeling, some things your partner may be feeling, and some specific challenges you may go through during treatments.

How you might be feeling

- Worried about whether your chosen treatment is the "right/best one"
  - This is natural: we want whatever treatment you're doing to be successful, so your brain starts doing what it is hardwired to do—seek safety. I found myself wondering at certain points whether we should reach out to another clinic for a second opinion on our case. For me, a mantra really helped when I felt that way—I would stop and say to myself ten times: "We've chosen the best option for treatment, and we have a great medical team to support us." It sounds sort of hokey, but I found this helped me press pause on those anxious thoughts.
- Overwhelmed by advice from friends or (more likely) the internet
  - Logically my brain knew that I should take advice from random internet influencers and blog posts with a grain

    of salt, but that's easier said than done —we were willing to do *anything* possible to have a baby.

- Compelled to constantly check how your partner is feeling
    - During our first round of IVF, I realized while sitting on the couch watching TV I had asked Olivia "How are you feeling?" three times in the course of twenty minutes. She was gracious enough not to smack me across the face, but I quickly recognized I had to notice and stop myself from checking in excessively. This can add more stress at an already stressful time!
- Upset by what your partner has to endure
    - Not only was it hard to give Olivia shots, the IVF shots also made her feel miserable. By the last few days before egg retrieval, she mostly spent hours on the couch in various states of discomfort. This was hard! I wanted the treatment to work, but ALSO didn't want to see her in pain.
- If doing IVF, overwhelmed by the planning and execution
    - Finally, as I outlined at the start of this chapter, there are a lot of logistics to fertility treatment, particularly IVF. Making my checklists and doing the preparation actually felt good in a way as I felt more in control, but it's still a lot to deal with.

HOW YOUR PARTNER MIGHT BE FEELING

Likewise, your partner will experience new challenges as treatment begins.

- Exhaustion, discomfort, and irritation
  - By the time we were several days into IVF shots, Olivia was incredibly uncomfortable and had to spend hours each day propped up on the couch with heating pads, cooling pads, and ibuprofen. She had headaches, and felt extreme pressure as her ovaries pumped up way past normal size.
- Hyper awareness of every sensation in her body and tempted to analyze what it means
  - During one cycle of IVF, Olivia kept feeling what she described as "pings" or "zaps" around where her ovaries are, and we of course were tempted to analyze them — was it a good sign that more follicles and eggs are growing? Or was it something to be concerned about?
- Annoyance that you get the "easy" part
  - Hey, it's not a slight against you or a criticism—it's just true! We're generally not the ones taking multiple shots every day!
- Overwhelmed by pressure due to feeling that success is "on her"
  - All of the above can be exacerbated significantly by the feeling that success or failure rests almost entirely on her.

~ ~ ~

I hoisted the bags out of the trunk and headed toward the back door. I hadn't planned to stop for groceries on my way home, but driving to work that morning, I'd heard a guest on a podcast talk about how she believed that going gluten-free helped her conceive and have a healthy baby. A bit of Googling later, I was hook-line-and-sinker convinced that eliminating gluten had to be the magical key to success.

I had it all planned out: I'd go to the grocery store, get a bunch of great gluten-free things, bring them home, and then tell Olivia all about what I'd learned. Then—voila! We were already stocked up, and I'd go gluten-free too. The way some of the things I'd read online made it sound, going gluten-free was probably just something I should do as well anyway. It seemed like a panacea for just about any ailment.

I spread the items out on the kitchen island: gluten-free crackers, gluten-free pasta, gluten-free cookies, gluten-free frozen pizza, gluten-free cereal and granola and bread. It was a bonanza! I started to cook dinner (gluten-free pasta, naturally) and awaited her return from work.

A few minutes later, I heard her familiar call as she walked in the back door.

"Hi love, I'm home!"

"Hi love," I returned. "Check out what I got at the store…"

Olivia walked into the kitchen and looked at the mountain of boxes and bags on the island. She wrinkled her nose and furrowed her eyebrows.

"Um…what is all this? Gluten-free crackers?"

I must have looked slightly wild-eyed as I excitedly explained to her all the things I had read that day.

"...and I think cutting out gluten will probably help get rid of my dandruff too!" I concluded a few minutes later.

Blinded by my excitement, I barely noticed her growing look of concern.

"But…this all looks gross, and I already feel like crap from these stupid medications without having to eat these bland crackers…look at all the weird ingredients in these, anyway," her voice was getting louder as she looked at me out of the corner of her eye. "And we asked the doctor already about any dietary changes and she didn't recommend any. We already eat healthy, we barely eat any gluten, and this is the craziest thing I've ever heard! I'm going upstairs to

change. And if gluten-free pasta is the only thing on the menu, then I'll have something else to eat!"

As Olivia climbed the stairs, I slunk toward the stove with my tail between my legs. I tossed out the pot of gluten-free pasta and looked for something else to cook. She was working so hard for us already—how had I let myself get so wrapped up in this gluten-free thing?

~ ~ ~

MR. DOOFUS AND MR. DEBONAIR: WHAT TO SAY AND WHAT NOT TO SAY TO YOUR PARTNER DURING FERTILITY TREATMENT

As you can see from my not-so-smooth move with the gluten-free food, sometimes things we do or say that we THINK are helpful…actually come off the total opposite way. But how do you know the difference? Well, let's take a moment and meet two imaginary men: Mr. Doofus, and Mr. Debonair, both of whose partners are undergoing fertility treatment, to illustrate and educate. Mr. Debonair always knows the right thing to say…Mr. Doofus on the other hand…well, you'll see.

- Scenario 1: The men's partners are telling them how rotten they're feeling from all the shots and hormones.
    - Mr. Doofus says: "It can't be that bad, and after all don't worry, it's only a few more days."
    - Mr. Debonair understands how hard it must be and wants to make sure he acknowledges it, so he says: "I can see how challenging this is for you physically and emotionally. I know I'm not going through the same

thing, but I can tell it is hard on you. Would you like some tea or to just veg out on the couch?"

- Scenario 2: The men's partners come home in tears after a colleague announces she's pregnant in the middle of a staff meeting.
    - Mr. Doofus says: "It's ok, we'll be the next ones! Take a deep breath and calm down."
    - Mr. Debonair can see his partner is really upset, so he listens quietly and pays attention to what she's saying for several minutes to understand how she's feeling then says: "That really sucks. It must have been hard to sit and listen to that. I'm sorry you had to go through it."
- Scenario 3: The men's partners share how they feel defeated, are convinced the treatments won't work, and are worried they'll never become parents.
    - Mr. Doofus says: "Come on, you know this work will pay off, we'll have a baby for sure! And if this doesn't work, we can always do another treatment."
    - Mr. Debonair knows that simply pushing his partner to be positive or to think about the next treatment might minimize how she is feeling or make it seem like he's giving up on the treatment they're doing right now, so he says: "I'm scared this treatment might not work too. I'm not giving up on it, I just really want us to become parents."
- Scenario 4: The men's partners are upset because after a monitoring appointment, the doctor calls and says their follicles are not growing as quickly as hoped.
    - Mr. Doofus says: "Don't be sad! It'll be ok! Cheer up!"

- Mr. Debonair knows that just saying to cheer up isn't really going to make her feel any better, so he says: "That's really hard news, especially because I know how much you're doing and how hard you're working and everything you're enduring for this treatment."

No one's perfect. There were certainly many times where I probably acted and sounded more like Mr. Doofus. But hopefully these small samples give an idea of how to put your most debonair foot forward.

~ ~ ~

The next evening, I stopped at the grocery store again on my way home. This time, I raced directly past the gluten-free section to the chocolate section. Olivia has always been a fan of anything involving chocolate and peanuts or coconut. I grabbed a couple extra nice artisanal chocolate bars, didn't even check if they contained anything with gluten, and then went to the card aisle. I grabbed a blank card with a nice heart design on the front, and wrote an apology note on the interior.

Half an hour later, she was coming in the back door again.

"Hi love, I'm home," she called.

This time, she walked in to see a card and the chocolate on the kitchen island. She read the card and turned to me, a tender look in her eyes.

"I'm really sorry, love," I said. "I didn't mean to make this even harder than it is already. Forget the gluten-free stuff. I hope you'll forgive me."

Olivia smiled and came over to give me a kiss on the cheek.

"I'll forgive you, but first I've got to make sure—is that pasta on the stove gluten-free?"

I laughed. "I SWEAR it's chock-full of gluten!"

~ ~ ~

DEALING WITH GIVING SHOTS

Next up, let's talk about shots. If you end up doing IVF, your partner will have to take many injections, potentially a couple dozen or more over a single cycle. Depending on your particular situation, the number may be even higher. In our case, Olivia had to take a daily blood thinner injection which really upped her numbers: after our second IVF cycle, I did some quick estimation and reckoned she had taken somewhere on the order of 350 shots in all.

Before we dive in, you may be somewhat surprised (as I certainly was) that you and your partner are "allowed" to give all of these shots in your own home. Neither of us had ever received a shot outside of the doctor's office, though we later remembered friends and family members with diabetes who were old pros at giving themselves shots of insulin. Rest assured that many thousands (if not millions) of couples have learned to administer IVF injections successfully. Your fertility clinic should offer ample support as to the process (like the handy e-learning course ours gave us), and there are also many videos and articles online which explain the process in detail (just be sure to check and use reputable sources such as videos posted by hospitals and fertility clinics).

First and foremost, you'll want to figure out *who's going to give the shots*? Your partner may want to do it on her own to be in control of the process, in which you're just the cheerleader. However, your partner might be (understandably) hesitant about administering shots to herself. IVF medicines also generally don't go in the arm—they go in the lower abdomen, upper thigh, and in some cases, in the lower back/upper buttock area. None of these are the most comfortable place to self-inject, though again many women do it successfully. Your partner may also just be more comfortable dealing with the pain of the shot without having to worry about jabbing it in. Regardless, the takeaway is the same: you may find yourself designated shot giver! We determined early on that Olivia did not want to self-administer, so I rolled up my sleeves, washed my hands with antibacterial soap, and paid close attention to a crash course in syringes, vials, and injections.

Below, I offer my shot prep checklist—I made this simple list up when we first started IVF just to help me ensure I didn't miss anything. You can find a downloadable single page copy at TheIVFDad.com. My adrenaline was really running as I prepared those first few shots, so having this list helped me feel much more confident in what I was doing. Use it or add to it if it's helpful for you, and of course, always follow all of the instructions that your doctor or clinic provides.

- Step 1: Wash your hands vigorously up to the wrists for 30 seconds in warm water with antibacterial soap, dry thoroughly.
- Step 2: Get EVERYTHING out and prepared—all vials, syringes, rubbing alcohol or other antiseptic swabs, sterile gauze, soap, towels, bandages(s) and any "support" items like a fun playlist.
- Step 3: Assemble syringes, open vials, swab vial tops with a rubbing alcohol pad after opening.
- Step 4: If any medicines require mixing, check directions and mix accordingly, then fill syringes with proper dose. Dispose of any needles used for mixing if necessary. For any medicines with pre-loaded syringes, ensure the dose is set to the correct amount.
- Step 5: Double check one final time to ensure all doses are correct and syringes are loaded and ready. Wash hands again if you've touched anything other than the sterile materials.

- Step 6: Prepare the injection location by thoroughly swabbing the area with rubbing alcohol.
- Step 7: Ensure your sterile gauze square and bandage are open and out of packages.
- Step 8: Take a deep breath!
- Step 9: Administer shots, then place sterile gauze over the injection site, applying light pressure.
- Step 10: Place needles/syringes immediately into a disposable sharps container.

Remember, preparation is the key! You'll probably still feel a bit anxious the first time you administer shots, but it gets easier. And if you aren't the shot giver—be a great cheerleader for your partner if it helps her.

THE IVF HUNGER GAMES—BACK TO THE YO-YO

After retrieving eggs from your partner, there is natural attrition (that is, diminishing numbers) as you wait on those eggs to fertilize and grow. Thus, waiting for embryos to grow during an IVF cycle is tremendously stressful.

Before we started IVF, I had no idea this attrition happened. I figured the process put a tight control around these mysterious processes—Olivia's eggs would come out, mix with my sperm, and voila! We'd have a number of embryos to implant which would surely give us great odds of success. But as we know from earlier, the average success rate for an IVF cycle, according to the CDC, is somewhere in the range of 25-45% depending on your situation. There are still many steps from growing eggs to creating and successfully implanting embryos, and at each step things can go wrong.

This can feel like a return to the infertility yo-yo. You may undergo an egg retrieval and feel great after retrieving 20 eggs from your partner, then find out the next day only 5 of those eggs have fertilized. It's total whiplash—this brings us back to the "IVF Hunger Games" I mentioned earlier. The numbers keep dwindling and you hope as many eggs and embryos as possible survive! Knowing this will happen doesn't make it easier, but it does prepare you for the mental challenge. Let's look at the different "hurdles" along the IVF cycle where the Hunger Games take place.

- Hurdle 1: Growing and Retrieving Eggs

As we headed into our first egg retrieval, our doctor said they were hoping for somewhere in the range of 10-14 eggs based on ultrasound checks. In the end, the RE came out and announced they had retrieved eight eggs. Initially, this was a let down. After all, Olivia had endured physical and emotional discomfort growing those eggs, and we raised our expectations based on the estimate of 10-14 eggs.

But as with so much else in this process, there's wide variation and no such thing as "normal." For one woman, retrieving six eggs may be a fantastic result—while another woman may get 30 or more eggs. In the end, we appreciated our RE setting realistic expectations for us, but this was our first experience of the crazy ups and downs in the days following an egg retrieval.

- Hurdle 2: Embryo Fertilization

As we left our egg retrieval, our nurse told us she'd call the next day to let us know how many eggs had been fertilized. In our case, we were quite fortunate during our first cycle—all eight eggs fertilized. Our nurse told us this was fantastic, but unusual; generally not all eggs fertilize.

According to Natalist.com, the average fertilization rate is somewhere around 70-80%, but again—this is just an average, and each couple is different. You want as many eggs to fertilize as possible, but attrition at this point is expected. If you have a very low fertilization rate, the doctor may suggest additional testing or may be able to provide some idea of potential root causes—and depending on the situation, may suggest procedures like ICSI which could potentially help.

- Hurdle 3: Embryo Growth

The final hurdle is the most difficult. Once you have fertilized embryos, they are left to grow over the next 4-5 days. The embryologist in the lab checks their progress daily, and the clinic should keep you informed of any changes. According to the Reproductive Medicine Associates of Connecticut, on average, only about 30-50% of embryos grow normally and sufficiently to become healthy blastocysts which are candidates for transfer/implantation. So if you had a great yield and 10 embryos fertilized, it's normal to make it to transfer day with 3-5 usable embryos. If you have fewer embryos to start with, you can see that the math gets harder. In our case, the eight fertilized embryos left us with four viable candidates on transfer day—a pretty typical rate, which we and our doctor were pleased with.

What causes this attrition? There are two possibilities: first, some of the embryos simply stop growing over the course of the five days. This can be due to genetic abnormalities or other factors, but it is normal for some embryos to stop progressing. Second, some embryos do grow but are lower quality and thus not great candidates for transfer. How does the lab determine this? Embryos[2] have a visual grading system that the embryologist uses to gauge quality by examining them under a microscope. Healthy and normal looking embryos get a higher grade, and embryos that are growing abnormally get a lower grade. There are different grading systems, so ask your lab what they use if you want to know more.

The most common system (called the Robinson blastocyst grading scale) grades embryos using a combination of a number and one or two

---

[2] I'm using the term "embryo" here for simplicity, but scientifically, once the embryo survives to day 5 it has usually moved from "embryo" stage to "blastocyst" stage.

letters, so you'll see grades like 2A, 4BA, 3BC, 4B, or 5AB. The numbers generally run 1-5 with higher being more favorable, and the letters consist of A, B, and C, with A being the best and C being lower quality. So a grade like 5AA is highly favorable in terms of overall quality, while a 2CC is not as favorable and thus less likely to implant successfully.

As you get closer to a possible embryo transfer, your clinic should keep you informed as to how many potential viable embryos you have. On transfer day, you'll get a complete explanation of your embryos, their grades, and a recommendation of which one (or in some limited cases multiple embryos—remember the section in the last chapter about single vs multiple egg transfers) your doctor believes has the best chance for implantation and growth.

Does the Hunger Games analogy make more sense now? It's entirely normal to start with, say, 15 eggs retrieved, and end up with just three or four viable embryos after five days of growth.

Given these hurdles, you may come to the end of an IVF cycle and not have any viable embryos to transfer. This is obviously a huge letdown. You and your partner have both made a tremendous sacrifice and put in a huge effort without the return you hoped for.

Your doctor should schedule a follow up to debrief what may have happened and should be prepared to explain what, if anything, could be done differently in the future. Their best answer may be that you just have to try again and hope for one good embryo—but at the very least, they should debrief the cycle and explain your options going forward.

~ ~ ~

"Ok," the doctor said cheerily, "let's take a look at your results."

The small office adjacent to the operating room was rather spartan. A calendar and a few stock photos of flowers were all that adorned the walls, and the only furniture was a small desk with one chair on one side and two chairs on the other. Transfer day was finally here. Olivia was fully in scrubs, ready to go and have an embryo implanted inside her in a few moments. I wasn't able to go in for the procedure itself, but was able to join in the waiting area as she prepared. We sat down at the little desk, nervously awaiting the doctor's next words.

The doctor took out a single sheet of paper from our file and placed it on the desk, twirling it around so that the paper was right side up for our viewing.

"So we should be very pleased with the results of this cycle. You'll remember that of the eight eggs retrieved, all eight fertilized. This list shows how those resulting embryos grew over the past five days. So you'll see that three of them arrested over time, here, here, and here."

"Arrested?" I asked.

"This means they stopped growing," the doctor continued, "which is normal. Not all embryos continue to grow, so we do anticipate some drop off in numbers. Now to turn to the remaining five embryos, two are lower quality, and three are higher quality. After reviewing with the embryologist, we'd recommend discarding the two of lower quality. They're not well-formed, and so probably not great candidates for a successful transfer."

"Ok," Olivia said, "so that means...discard...just get rid of them?"

"Correct," responded the doctor, "I know we want every embryo to make it, but we also want to be realistic. I want to ensure we're only transferring the highest quality embryos to give the best chance of success, and the literature shows that poorly graded embryos like these two are unlikely to implant and result in healthy pregnancies."

I looked over at Olivia. This all made perfect scientific sense, but just discarding two embryos seemed somehow wrong. We'd worked so hard for them. I could see her hesitating as well.

"Is that…what people typically do with lower-grade embryos?" she asked.

"That's right," said the doctor, "and I know that can be a complicated thing to think about. The other option would be to send these lower quality ones out for genetic testing and freeze them. Given their quality, they may be less likely to survive a freeze. I want to make sure you have all the information though and feel comfortable."

I mulled this over. "Why don't we talk about the three high-quality ones and maybe that will help us make sense of everything?"

"Of course," continued the doctor, "the positive news is we have three embryos that appear to be of good quality. Our lab is very picky about grading, but these have very strong grades: a 3AB, 4AB, and 4AA. I always want to ensure we're giving the best shot, so I would recommend that today we transfer the 4AA—the highest graded embryo. The other good news is that the remaining two can be frozen for later use."

"So we could be done, in other words?" she asked, "Like if this 4AA works, and we freeze the others, I could have two or three kids from this batch?"

"Knock on wood for good luck of course," the doctor smiled, "but that's right. So now that we've reviewed everything, how does this all sound to you both?"

"I guess I understand more now why it makes sense to discard the two lower grades since we have those three higher quality ones," Olivia said. "I guess it just feels like we're letting them go, but I know I have to think of this as a natural part of the process."

I felt the same way. It was sad to simply discard embryos. But we needed to give ourselves the best possible shot, and thankfully we now had one embryo to use and two in the bank. It was a lot more, and a lot more hope, than we had a few weeks prior.

"Alright then," the doctor said, "then there's just a few papers to sign, and then we'll head in. Olivia, I'll see you in the procedure room in just a moment."

As the doctor exited, Olivia and I exchanged looks. It was really happening. In just a few minutes, our little 4AA embryo would be deposited in her uterus. I could only hope that it would stick.

~ ~ ~

A DIGRESSION: DUMB THINGS PEOPLE WILL SAY

It's been an info-packed chapter thus far, so for a bit of levity, let's examine another topic that can be a real source of bonding for couples going through fertility treatment: the stupid things people say when they find out you're having trouble conceiving! I share this partly to commiserate, but also as fair warning. Hopefully we can all look back and laugh at how dumb some of these statements are. For now, try to laugh at how stupid they are, and rest assured you're not the only infertile couple who has heard them:

- "Just relax! When you least expect it, it will happen."
  - How you respond: "Fingers crossed!"
  - How you want to respond: "Yeah, nothing helps me relax like being ordered to relax!"
- "Are you sure it's not working? Maybe you're just not doing it right. Why don't you get a hot tub suite for a night and have some hot sex?
  - How you respond: *Cringing laugh*
  - How you want to respond: "Believe me, we've been doing it right. And hot tubs may hurt sperm quality, so that would be counterproductive."

- "The minute you go to see a fertility doctor, you'll get pregnant. Just wait and see!"
    - How you respond: "Hope you're right!"
    - How you want to respond: "Thanks, fortune teller. Do you offer a money back guarantee on your predictions?"
- "Pfft—I've got kids, and I'll trade ya. Enjoy the extra sleep while you can!"
    - How you respond: "Ha!"
    - How you want to respond: *Punch in face* "We've been trying to conceive for years. I'd trade my left nut to be waking up with a baby at two in the morning."
- "Have you tried this (position, supplement, essential oil, etc)? It worked for my niece's friend."
    - How you respond: "Maybe that's the key…"
    - How you want to respond: "Tell your niece's friend to go tell Dr. Oz about it, I don't care and we've tried everything."
- "I'm glad you at least have your dog!"
    - How you respond: "I know, he's the best."
    - How you want to respond: "Yeah, I love the dog but...does it look like a baby to you?"
- "Maybe the Universe is trying to tell you something."
    - How you respond: *Nodding with blank stare*
    - How you want to respond: "F&#& YOU"
- "Hey, you must be having a lot of sex, so not all bad right?"
    - How you respond: *Laughs*

  - How you want to respond: "Yes, nothing screams "hot and steamy" like having routinized sex at appointed times."
- "Remember, there are people who have things a lot worse."
  - How you respond: "Sure."
  - How you want to respond: "Thanks, Gandhi."

THE TWO WEEK WAIT

The two week wait needs no introduction. You likely already experienced it in the period before you started fertility treatments—maybe more times than you'd prefer to remember. And you already know how difficult those two weeks can be, spent living in between hope for a positive pregnancy test, and anxiety and fear about yet another cycle without success.

Those weeks are hard enough when trying to conceive the old-fashioned way, but I found the challenge was even more intense when we were doing IVF. Worst of all, you know for sure after an IUI or IVF that there's a chance your partner is pregnant, so your temptation to check in and monitor how she's feeling might be off the charts. In Olivia's case, two of her early pregnancy symptoms were burping (like full on Homer Simpson-esque belches), and having to pee almost non-stop.

Let's take a brief peek into Keegan's brain and hear what my inner monologue typically sounded like over the course of an hour during the two week wait.

- 1:00 pm
  - Hey, Olivia had an enormous burp after lunch. YES! Keep 'em rolling, the more burps the better, this has got to be a good sign.

- 1:05 pm
  - Wait though, what if the burps are just made up, like some crazy psychosomatic thing to trick us into thinking Olivia's pregnant? Or what if it's just because we had fajitas with lots of black beans? Were those burps as big as the ones after breakfast? This can't be good, maybe Olivia's not pregnant after all…
- 1:16 pm
  - This is such BS. It's so unfair. Other couples go off to an all-inclusive resort, spend all afternoon drinking margaritas, enjoy some romantic time back in their room, and come back pregnant. Meanwhile, here we are counting burps. What did we do to deserve this? Wait…do I hear a toilet flushing…please tell me that's Olivia going pee again!
- 1:25 pm
  - I wonder if she feels any burps coming on. Would she kill me if I go ask?
- 1:41 pm
  - We've given so much to this effort. Poor Olivia…dozens of shots and appointments. We started trying to have a baby three years ago. We could already have one baby and another on the way if we were normal. I just really, really hope this works.
- 1:52 pm
  - *Loud burp from down the hallway* *WOOHOO!*

Get the picture? This back-and-forth in my brain basically played on repeat through each two week wait we've experienced, although it's gotten easier over time. I'd be lying if I claimed to have a trick to make the two week wait a breeze, and it's impossible to fully avoid some obsessive symptom-checking, but there were a few things we've done that made it at least a little easier.

First, we always tried to make a few plans during the two week wait to ensure we were busy and had things to look forward to. One time we took a long weekend and went to Savannah in the middle of it, another time we went on an overnight trip closer to home. We usually went to the movies at least once. While we still spent plenty of time obsessing over symptoms and counting down the hours, having some planned breaks along the way really helped.

Second, we made a plan in advance about whether we'd do an at-home pregnancy test, and stuck to our decision. As you might know, it's possible after an IUI or IVF embryo transfer to use at-home pregnancy tests to get a positive or negative result before your partner's hCG beta test via blood work at the clinic. The pro to testing early: you and your partner can get an idea of the result before the beta and start preparing to manage your reaction, whatever the outcome. The con: as explained above, the home pregnancy tests do not provide an exact hCG level, so you don't know if the hCG is going up properly, or how high it actually is. Olivia and I decided not to use home pregnancy tests for this very reason—we wanted the certainty of the clinic's test (though we were tempted at times!)

DEALING WITH A NEGATIVE BETA

Unfortunately, no fertility treatment offers guaranteed success. Many couples get to the day of the hCG beta and receive the news that the cycle did not result in a pregnancy. Remember, the overall rate for a successful healthy pregnancy after IVF, according to the CDC's data, is somewhere between 25-45% depending on your particular situation. But there's no mincing words here—getting a "you're not pregnant" call from the clinic is devastating. You've put in a tremendous amount of physical and emotional effort into the treatment and probably raised your hopes of success after so much heartbreak.

Anticipate being tempted to fall back on our usual ways of reacting and thinking. You might find yourself back in "fix-it" mode Googling more information about treatments, or trying to cheer up your partner by saying things like "Don't worry, we can always try again" instead of acknowledging her feelings. There is time for looking ahead later, but first ensure you and your partner have space to just be sad and disappointed.

Once you've taken some time, you can start to look ahead to debriefing with your doctor and considering what steps might be next. The doctor may not have a concrete answer as to what happened, but you can bring the following list of questions to your debrief to ensure that conversation is productive:

- Do you have a sense of why the cycle didn't work?
- How typical was this outcome given our health, age, and other factors?
- Does the result change your assessment of what course of treatment gives us the best shot at success?
- Is there any additional testing that either of us could or should undergo to provide more information about why the cycle didn't work?
- Would you consider making any changes or additions to our treatment in future cycles?
- What are our options from here?

REVIEWING WAYS TO SUPPORT YOURSELF/YOUR PARTNER

This chapter has covered a lot of ground. Undergoing fertility treatment is no joke, right? It forces us to deal with an extremely high level of stress and anxiety. Be patient with yourself and your partner, and return to these strategies often. They still may feel like new and uncomfortable tactics given how different they are from what we are typically encouraged to do as males—but hopefully you're seeing some of the benefits, and starting to build them as habits.

Of course, with fertility treatment, there's always another layer of challenge ahead. It would be amazing to live in a world where getting a positive beta meant you and your partner had a blissful nine months ahead of you ending with a healthy baby. But we (and sadly, many others) know all too well this isn't always the case.

A brief warning: the next chapter delves into miscarriage and pregnancy loss, which is an incredibly difficult, but sadly common experience. If you'd rather skip over this content for now, feel free to jump ahead.

CHAPTER 7

WHEN THINGS GO WRONG

A brief warning: this chapter focuses on miscarriage and pregnancy loss. This is a common but obviously incredibly difficult experience. If you're not in a space to read about this topic, feel free to skip ahead.

"Common side effects may include nausea, heartburn, skin rash, joint discomfort, headache, anxiety, and digestive upset."

The third pharmaceutical commercial in a row blared from the TV in the corner of the waiting room. Olivia and I were captive and growing restless, now having endured over half an hour of mind-numbing morning talk show content. I wasn't sure which was worse, the stupefying gossip about which celebrity was seen gently brushing the hand of another celebrity at a swanky restaurant last weekend, or the incessant commercials aimed at a demographic of people who evidently had unending lists of physical ailments and wouldn't mind risking a litany of equally nasty side effects to get rid of them.

As if all this wasn't unpleasant enough, we were waiting on a major milestone: our 12-week ultrasound. And we were, frankly, wracked with anxiety.

After our miscarriage and that dark December night at the hospital for the D&C, we waited a couple months and returned to our clinic to try again. We had frozen embryos from our prior IVF cycle, and while the loss had been devastating, we learned how common miscarriages were. Our hope was it had been simply "one of those things."

Thus, on a cold February day, we went in for another embryo transfer, and ten days later, got another call to confirm that Olivia was indeed pregnant. Our reaction was starkly different from the celebratory Halloween night a few months prior. Of course we were pleased, but the happiness was blunted by a deep fear. Now we knew how traumatic a pregnancy loss was, and it was impossible not to feel stressed about the possibility of experiencing it again.

And so, it was with some amount of surprise and amazement that we cruised through our 8 and 10 week ultrasounds at the IVF clinic. At each appointment, we'd enter the ultrasound room anxiously, our breathing shallow and hearts pounding. Olivia and I would clutch each other's hand tightly as the sonographer came in and inserted the ultrasound wand. And each time, we saw a flickering heartbeat and breathed a sigh of relief.

After our 10 week appointment, we reached a critical milestone: "graduating" from the IVF clinic. The clinic was nearly empty on a late weekday afternoon. Despite the great news we'd just received, this step of leaving the clinic for what we hoped would be the last time felt anticlimactic.

Having graduated, we found ourselves back in the pool of "normal" pregnancies, which led us to Olivia's usual OB office and to the awful string of commercials. It was now late spring.

Looking around the waiting room, there were several other women at various stages of pregnancy (at least the ones who were far along enough to show). Preparing for this appointment, the regular OB reassured us that given the results of our early ultrasounds at our IVF clinic, and the earlier miscarriage notwithstanding, we would get the typical treatment for any other pregnant couple. It was easy to understand from a scientific perspective why this was the case, but we certainly didn't feel like a normal pregnant couple after what we'd been through. I looked at the other pregnant women and wondered. How did she get pregnant? Have her and her partner ever experienced a miscarriage?

Even with the reassuring early ultrasounds, we still felt a rush of nerves as we sat and waited. At last, as one talk show ended and another began, an ultrasound tech entered the waiting room and called Olivia's name.

I squeezed her hand. The clinic was busy, and patients clogged the hallways as we paced back to the ultrasound room. We passed a pregnant woman pushing her two older kids in a stroller.

"Alright," said the tech as we took a right to enter the ultrasound room. "So you're here for a 12 week ultrasound correct? We'll get started, and we'll take a couple of measurements today that help us assess risk for certain birth defects. You can pull your shirt up to your chest, ma'am. And sir, you can sit right in the chair by the door and watch on the monitor overhead."

Olivia looked surprised at first. At the IVF clinic, the ultrasounds were done via a vaginal wand—the growing little baby was too small for a traditional ultrasound done over the abdomen.

"This is a big step," she told the ultrasound tech. "We did IVF, so we haven't done a regular ultrasound yet."

"Yep," responded the tech, business-like and dry in her efficient manner. "The baby should be big enough to see via abdominal scan by now."

I settled in the chair as the sonographer applied a large globule of clear goop to Olivia's abdomen and placed the transducer under her belly button, moving it around to find a clear view of our baby. After a moment, I saw the outline of the baby come into focus. Almost instantaneously, a rush of nervous hormones slammed into my chest.

Time slowed down as I felt a dizzying headrush. Over the next three seconds, the following realizations crashed into my brain: Something was different than at the IVF clinic. Something wasn't right. I could see the grayish form of the baby, but at the IVF clinic, we'd seen a little blinking heart right in the tiny chest. We'd seen the flicker. There was no flicker now.

I stood up. The ultrasound tech was silent for an excruciating moment.

"I'm not seeing bloodflow. I'm not seeing a heartbeat," the tech stated, still utterly dry and business-like.

I rushed across the room to Olivia and grabbed her hand, stammering: "No. Not again. Please, please no."

She unleashed a guttural cry at the ultrasound tech: "Get OUT and get the doctor. NOW."

The ultrasound tech rushed out.

Sitting on the cold ultrasound table, Olivia crumpled forward into my arms. We grasped each other, the only solid thing it felt like we had to hold onto in that moment. And we sobbed for another baby we'd never meet.

~ ~ ~

Those minutes in the ultrasound room were the most painful experience of my life. One miscarriage was a tragedy, but a second just five months later? It seemed like the universe was out to get us, taking our already bruised and fragile selves and beating us down even further. Later that night, sitting alone again in a small room on the labor and delivery of the ward of the hospital, as Olivia was anesthetized enduring yet another D&C down the hall, I felt numb and empty. Sadly, no anesthesia could take away the emotional savagery the day had wrought on us.

While I wish no one ever had to endure such trauma, we had learned a lot about pregnancy loss since our first miscarriage. If you and your partner go through a pregnancy loss, the most important thing is to grieve, but it's also critical to understand some facts about miscarriage to help you understand that you're experiencing something extremely common and over which you usually have very little control.

MISCARRIAGE MYTHBUSTING

So, let's start by looking at the facts. We really didn't know much of anything about miscarriages until we went through it ourselves. While nothing can take the pain away from suffering a pregnancy loss, knowing some facts and dispelling some myths did help with the healing process, and allowed us to be easier on ourselves.

- Myth: Miscarriage is rare.
    - Fact: The Mayo Clinic estimates that somewhere in the range of 10-20% of pregnancies end in a loss. About 85% of these losses occur within the first trimester (the first 12 weeks).
- Myth: Miscarriages can be prevented.
    - Fact: While there are some conditions like structural problems in the uterus that can be treated, current research suggests roughly half of all miscarriages are the result of genetic abnormalities in the fetus which you and your partner have no control over.
- Myth: Miscarriages "just happen," and there's nothing we can do about them.
    - Fact: While many miscarriages occur due to factors out of our control, there can be underlying conditions like autoimmune disorders or structural issues with your partner's uterus or cervix which may raise the risk. Some

of these factors can be addressed by a doctor to decrease the risk of future losses. Thus, it's important to discuss all possibilities with your doctors after a pregnancy loss.

- Myth: Injuries/stress/caffeine can cause miscarriages.
  - Fact: There are many myths and old wives tales out there about what causes pregnancy loss. A doctor friend once told me he had an elderly female patient who once told him she had a miscarriage when she was younger because she "went on a bumpy car ride." It can be easy for you and your partner to obsess and blame yourselves but know that typical experiences like taking a fall, having a (normal) intake of coffee, or everyday stress is unlikely to have had any role in the loss.
- Myth: Having a miscarriage means you're more likely to have another, or to have difficulty having a healthy pregnancy.
  - Fact: Most women who have miscarriages can go on to have healthy pregnancies. Only about 2% of women experience two consecutive pregnancy losses, and only about 0.5% experience three consecutive losses, per the Yale School of Medicine.

Now that you're armed with some knowledge about pregnancy loss, let's take some time to understand what happens specific to fertility treatment with miscarriages.

Blood Draws and Beta Limbo

For many women, bleeding is the first sign of miscarriage. Because most pregnancy losses happen quite early, this can happen very suddenly on its own. As we reviewed earlier though, most fertility clinics have the woman conduct an hCG blood test, or "beta", about 10-14 days after an

IUI or embryo transfer. After the first beta confirms the pregnancy, your partner will probably have another blood draw two days later to see how the hCG level is progressing. It should be roughly doubling every 36-48 hours.

If the hCG number does not double, your clinic will draw another beta in two more days. It's important to note that some pregnancies simply don't follow the doubling rule and turn out entirely healthy and normal. However, an hCG level that rises too slowly may indicate the pregnancy is not progressing properly.

This can lead to a very stressful situation we call "beta limbo." We experienced beta limbo during our first pregnancy. Our first beta came back to confirm the pregnancy, but then on the second beta, the hCG level failed to double. Cruelly, the third beta nearly doubled, which gave some hope. Subsequent betas continued to creep up, but never fully doubled, even after several additional weeks. It was impossible to tell the outcome until we finally reached a stage at which the clinic could perform an ultrasound. After several excruciating weeks in limbo, an ultrasound confirmed that the pregnancy was not successful—the embryo had implanted but resulted in a "blighted ovum" or empty gestational sac without a fetus. The miscarriage did not start on its own, so the gestational sac was continuing to grow slightly, hence the very slow rise in hCG that kept the limbo going.

It's unlikely to find yourself in quite such a degree of uncertainty as our story. The clinic will keep in close touch and monitor the situation closely with you if you are in beta limbo, but the clinic simply may not have any concrete answers right away. Even after four betas, our doctor and nurses didn't know how things were going to resolve during our first pregnancy. They were direct and let us know the slow hCG growth was not a promising sign, but there was nothing definitive they could know at that point. An ultrasound would be the only way to determine for sure, which wasn't possible until at least six weeks gestation.

In other cases, there may be more clear cut indications about what is happening. The hCG level might grow slowly for the first beta and then start doubling normally, which could well indicate you're on your way to a healthy normal pregnancy. The hCG level might stagnate or start to fall, which unfortunately would indicate a likely impending miscarriage.

Beta limbo is an awful place to be. Use the strategies listed elsewhere in the book to manage it as best you can. If you have questions, don't hesitate to ask the clinic. Later in this chapter, we'll look at what options are available to you and your partner if unfortunately the resolution of your beta limbo is a pregnancy loss.

Chemical Pregnancies

Before looking at treatment options and how to deal with the emotions if you face a pregnancy loss, let's briefly cover some other scenarios.

As covered earlier, modern home pregnancy tests are quite advanced and allow you to detect pregnancy extremely early—sometimes even within 5-8 days of an embryo transfer. A downside is since the vast majority of pregnancy losses occur early in pregnancy, it's possible to get a positive pregnancy test on these home kits, but then experience a very early miscarriage. Because there are usually few symptoms at this point, and the bleeding may seem like a heavy period, these are often called "chemical pregnancies." In other words—the only "evidence" or "symptom" of the pregnancy was the chemical presence of hCG.

You may also experience something like this if you have a very low beta hCG blood draw. If the level of hCG is present but extremely low, and especially if it stagnates, falls, or rises slowly, the clinic may express that the pregnancy may not continue successfully. Your partner's body may simply start to bleed on its own.

If you search in that awful breeding ground of the internet, you'll quickly see some debate as to whether chemical pregnancies "count as a loss." My take? If you go through this, you definitely experienced a real loss. You and your partner found out that you were pregnant, and then the pregnancy did not work out. You still deserve time to grieve, and are justified in feeling devastated. Further reason not to spend too much time on the internet when it comes to these issues!

UNDERSTANDING TREATMENT OPTIONS

If you've reached the point where a miscarriage is expected or a failed pregnancy is diagnosed, the situation will need to be resolved in some way, and the clinic will likely present a few options if the miscarriage process has not started on its own. It goes without saying that this is a gut wrenching, stressful, and traumatic time. Shortly we'll look at dealing with the emotions of pregnancy loss, but first let's understand what the treatment options may be.

Your clinic's role at this point is to help your partner and you "manage" the miscarriage—it's a cold and clinical term, but they need to support in ensuring the fetus safely leaves your partner's body without causing any complications, which could put your changes of future conceptions at risk, or put your partner's health at risk.

One option is to wait for the miscarriage to occur naturally, if it is safe to do so. Another option is for your partner to take medication to essentially "jumpstart" bleeding and get the miscarriage started. Another option, if appropriate and necessary, is to undergo a dilation and curettage (D&C) or dilation and evacuation (D&E) surgery to remove the fetus.

It goes without saying that your doctor should discuss all the pros and cons of these options, explain which one they recommend in your situation, and provide lots of information to help you make the decision that is right for you. And indeed, your doctor may not recommend certain of these options if they are not viable given the particulars of your case.

In our case, the miscarriages simply would not start on their own. For our first miscarriage, Olivia opted to try the medication method, but unfortunately the meds failed to start the process. This is why we ended up at the hospital for a D&C. With our second loss, the pregnancy was too far along to wait things out, so we opted for a D&C to resolve things as quickly as possible. I sincerely wish that you never have to engage in this conversation—but hopefully the information herein will prepare you and your partner if you do face it.

Ectopic Pregnancies

A final condition to note, which is slightly different than the ones above: ectopic pregnancy occurs when the embryo implants somewhere outside the uterus—usually in the fallopian tube. This is relatively rare, only occurring in 2% or less of pregnancies. Unfortunately, it is not possible for the fetus to survive an ectopic pregnancy, so they result in a miscarriage.

An ectopic pregnancy still releases hCG, so you would initially find out you and your partner are expecting. However, the level of hCG usually rises quite slowly with an ectopic pregnancy. Thus, with fertility treatments and beta draws, your clinic may identify a possible ectopic early on. Without such close monitoring, symptoms of an ectopic pregnancy usually show up within the first trimester of pregnancy, and include pelvic or abdominal pain, or vaginal bleeding.

If your partner has an ectopic pregnancy, the clinic will likely offer some options for resolution depending on the particular situation. An ectopic can be resolved via surgery or medication that can stop the pregnancy from progressing. Obviously in this case, discuss the options with your doctor, who will help you understand and make a decision about what to pursue. However, the options may be more limited and the surgery can require more recovery time, so the management of an ectopic may look slightly different than the options described above.

~ ~ ~

A couple weeks after our first miscarriage, I wandered out to the garage on a Saturday morning and started lugging a large box toward the house.

Olivia and I had spent much of the past weeks in a daze. There were mornings when I'd wake up, yawn lazily enjoying that brief moment of timeless blankness immediately after waking. Then suddenly, reality came crashing back—we're not expecting anymore. We're back at square one. We tried to keep ourselves busy, but there were many stretches where even doing something we normally enjoyed just felt like…well, nothing. Emptiness.

And we were in yet another waiting game. We had to wait for the hCG level in Olivia's blood to fully go down to zero before meeting with the doctor to talk about resuming treatment.

Yet something on that Saturday morning drew me to the large box in the garage. It contained the parts for a day bed we'd ordered to go in the bedroom that we'd chosen to become a nursery.

"So I was thinking maybe I'll put this together," I half-heartedly said, "And put it in…the room. I don't know. Am I crazy?" I couldn't quite bring myself to call it the nursery.

"I don't know if I'm ready for that," she replied.

I didn't know if I was ready either. I truly wondered if I was crazy. The future-nursery had become a symbol of everything we didn't have. Ever since the miscarriage, the door to that room sat closed tightly. It was filled with boxes. It was the one room in the house we hadn't painted. Putting together this day bed and placing it in that room seemed like foolish, impossible wishful thinking.

"I know," I responded. "I honestly don't know why I brought this in. I guess if we can't do anything right now to get closer to being parents, at least I can get out a stupid allen wrench."

"Well, I guess I know what you mean. It just feels so hopeless sometimes, like why even set that room up?"

"I know. Like we shouldn't even tempt the universe by assuming we'll ever get through this and have a baby..." I replied, musing sadly at how crazy infertility had made us sound.

Olivia considered the idea for a minute. "I suppose it can't hurt anything. And no matter what, we'll use the daybed for something someday."

A few hours later, the daybed sat fully assembled in the corner of the hopeful future-nursery. I had acquired a few small bruises along the way, having dropped the light gray frame on my toes.

Olivia entered as I finished adjusting the placement.

"Looks good, right?" I asked.

"It does," she replied. "I just really really hope we get to sit on it with a baby someday. Now let me get some sheets and pillows and make it look nice."

I put up the window shades. Light streamed into the room for the first time in weeks.

~ ~ ~

Questions to Get Answers To

After a pregnancy loss, you'll work with your clinic to fully assess what happened and whether you can do anything differently in a future treatment cycle. While you and your partner underwent lots of testing before even starting treatment, there may be additional tests worth completing before starting another round.

Be prepared to ask questions and advocate for yourself and your partner. While pregnancy loss is more common than most of us think, you've already overcome more than the average couple. Don't hesitate to respectfully but firmly press your doctor to explain whether any additional testing could yield useful information. Here are some questions you may want to ask, with explanations of why they're important.

- Can we test the miscarried fetus for genetic abnormalities?
    - Depending on the circumstances, it may be possible to conduct genetic testing on what in medical terms are called "the products of conception"—the tissue from the miscarried fetus. This is a very personal decision, one informed by many factors including you and your partner's faith. Doing the genetic testing, if you and your partner are open to it, can yield valuable information as to whether the fetus had inherent genetic issues. Why is this important? If the embryo had certain genetic issues to begin with, it may never have been capable of growing and surviving. Knowing this can provide some peace, and can also help you and your doctor decide whether to use PGT screening for future treatments (if you're doing IVF). If the testing does not reveal any abnormalities, that's also useful information—it rules out a genetic factor and lets the doctor focus on other issues that may have caused the loss, though as noted above—it's important to remember that in many cases, we may never know what caused a pregnancy loss.

- Have we tested fully for any structural uterine abnormalities?
    - As discussed earlier, a small percentage of women have structural abnormalities in their uterus. After a loss, it's a good time to ensure your doctor has fully assessed for any of these issues, as if present, they can make it difficult to implant and carry a healthy pregnancy. Some of these issues can also be treated if identified.
- Are there any other more specific blood tests for autoimmune, genetic, blood clotting, or other factors we should conduct?
    - Again, while you and your partner both should have had various blood testing before starting treatment, it's wise after a pregnancy loss to discuss any other testing with your doctor. Factors like autoimmune diseases, you or your partner carrying certain genetic markers, or your partner having blood clotting factors can cause issues with carrying healthy ongoing pregnancies.
- Should we consider pre-implantation genetic testing before a future cycle (if doing IVF)?
    - Finally, if you are doing IVF and have not used PGT screening, it may be wise to revisit this option with your doctor and consider if it could increase your chances for success.

It may be tempting to get back to treatment as soon as possible, but take the time to discuss these questions with your doctor. For Olivia and me, additional testing after our losses yielded useful information.

While we didn't test the remains from the first loss, we did have the second loss genetically tested. It turns out that it had a genetic abnormality called a trisomy, which meant it was unlikely to survive to a normal birth.

This was sad news, but at least gave us the comfort to know the situation was truly one that we had no control over.

Also, some additional blood testing revealed that Olivia had certain levels that could point to her having a blood clotting factor. Factors that increase the risk of blood clots can interfere with successful implantation and early pregnancy. While her results did not seem to indicate a severe issue, it led our doctor to recommend a blood thinner for future treatment. Truth be told, we'll never know for sure if the blood thinner was necessary, but we were happy to know that it may help, and we might never have had that option if not for the additional testing.

Arm yourself with as much information as possible—even if nothing new comes out, you'll go forward with greater confidence that you've done everything you could to have the best shot at success.

~ ~ ~

When we bought our house, we knew we loved the ample garden space, but didn't quite know the amount of work we were getting into. Between the weeding, planting, mulching, edging, raking, watering, and trimming, it seemed like from March through October of every year there was a constant list of things to be done outside.

While the results of our efforts were mixed (a failed plot of echinacea here, an overgrown row of asparagus there), each year we always had at least one thing we were really proud of: the amazing zinnia patch one year, the corner plot of snapdragons another.

In the weeks following our second miscarriage, spending time moving earth, digging holes, trimming weeds, and mixing compost became a sort of therapy. The fresh air and sunshine and warming breezes were certainly part of it, but simply being able to plant seeds, nurture them, and watch them grow also felt good. So much about our journey to parenthood was out of control, but at least I knew the zinnias were nearly foolproof.

One bright Saturday morning, preparing rows for seeds, I remembered something I'd read after our first miscarriage. A blogger suggested that doing a little ritual or ceremony to commemorate the pregnancy loss could be a great way to help feel more ready to move forward.

I don't know what made me remember that advice, but in truth, I had been struggling to let go of that lost pregnancy. We had made it so far. The idea of the baby was no longer abstract at the point we lost it; we had seen the little buds of arms and legs growing at the ultrasound prior to the bad one. Just at the point where it felt like we could finally almost breathe and enjoy the pregnancy, everything had gone wrong.

And so, as I knelt in the dirt, preparing to sow a packet of seeds that I hoped would grow into a beautiful assortment of flowers over the months ahead, I figured it was a good opportunity to put the advice to use.

I didn't prepare anything fancy. I simply let it unfold how it felt right.

I took a few deep breaths. I glanced up at the glowing sun.

And then I closed my eyes, and thought to myself: "Little one, I just want you to know that we loved you, and always will love you. Thank you for the time you spent with us. We'll never forget you."

I spent a few more seconds, just being still.

Then, I wiped away a few tears and sowed the seeds. Already, I felt lighter.

~ ~ ~

Moving Forward, not Moving On

Our pregnancy losses were easily the most difficult thing I've ever experienced. There were times when, knowing how painful a miscarriage was, I wondered whether continuing fertility treatment was worth it. There were days when hours went by in a blur, and it felt like putting one foot in front of the other was the only meaningful thing I could do.

When we shared the news of one of our miscarriages with a few friends and family, one person said something that's always stuck with me: "You don't have to move on from this, but with time, you will move forward." That quote captures the experience very well. We've never forgotten those losses, but we have found ways to put one foot in front of the other by doing things like the little memorial described above. We also benefited from talking to people, both friends, as well as counselors to help process those hard times.

The pregnancy you lost was real to you and your partner, and pressuring ourselves to "move on" can feel like we're minimizing the baby we lost and their memory. Thinking of "moving forward" instead reflects that you're not forgetting that difficult experience, but you are continuing your life.

My sincere hope to round out this chapter is that you never experience any of the things described here. But if you do, remember this: you are not alone. With patience, time, grace, and support, you can and will move forward.

CHAPTER 8

OTHER PATHS TO PARENTHOOD

"Are you Keegan?"

The woman waved as she emerged from her blue Subaru wagon. Olivia and I crossed the coffee shop parking lot, heading her way.

"Hi Trina, yes! It's nice to meet in person."

"Awesome to see you too," she went on, as her partner Joe got out of the car and shot us a warm smile. "I wasn't sure if I explained the right coffee shop, you know, there's another one just down the street, and we were running late getting the boys dressed and changed and we've got to swing by my mother's house afterwards, so we were grabbing things for her too, and we had to change a diaper before heading out the door of course, so it's been a busy few hours! Do we have everything Joe? Boys? Snacks? Books? Diaper bag? Ok, then let's head inside!"

We had connected on Facebook a few days prior through an advocacy group for families in our region who have children through adoption or fostering. Her messages gave the impression of a person who is extremely knowledgeable, passionate, and dedicated to helping families like her own. She and Joe had two young boys, both through adoption.

As Trina was speaking, rapidly moving from topic to topic while balancing a backpack in one arm, opening the rear car door with the other arm, unbuckling two car seats, and hoisting one of their sons into her arms, I could tell my impression was right. She seemed to have boundless energy. We followed them toward the coffee shop.

After the second miscarriage, Olivia and I had done a lot of thinking and talking about what might be next for us. We knew we wanted to return for another round of IVF, but we also decided we needed to look at other options for building our family. We had discussed adoption in passing, but never looked in depth at the process. A quick google search led me to the "Upstate Adoptive Families" Facebook group, and within a couple hours, Trina and I were exchanging messages. I explained our history and told her we were interested in learning more about the adoption process. She was more than happy to get together, offered to bring her own kids and partner along, and now, here we were, meeting just a couple days later.

We settled at a table and ordered some pastries and coffee. As they arranged their gear and little ones, I gazed at Trina and Joe's younger boy. He was just a few months old. He was in a deep, peaceful, almost angelic sleep, swaddled in his baby carrier. His older brother, who was four, doted on him, checking quietly to see how he was doing. I melted at this cute sight, but still felt a twinge of sadness, wondering if we'd ever have a baby of our own to love.

"Thanks again for meeting with us, and so quickly," Olivia piped up. "We really appreciate it."

"We're so happy to do it," Trina replied. "You know, Keegan told me what you guys have been through and we can talk all about the adoption process in a minute, but I have to tell you first—we were literally in your shoes just a few years ago. Fertility treatments, pregnancy losses—we've been there and done it all, just like you. So I just want you to know before we dig into the details that we get how hard it is. We wanted to bring our boys to show you how lucky we are—we have this amazing family now, which we spent lots of time wondering

if we'd ever have. I know you're probably feeling really low, but if you've made the choice to become parents, just know that there are lots of paths to get there."

I looked down at the boys again. The cuteness still gave warm and fuzzy feelings, but after hearing Trina's words, I felt the accompanying twinge of sadness receding ever so slightly. It was obvious how deeply in love Trina and Joe were with their family. I could start to envision Olivia and I being just as happy, even if we didn't know exactly what our path to parenthood would be.

~ ~ ~

PREGNANT OR PARENTS?

Driving home after meeting Trina, Joe and their boys, I felt a renewed optimism—something I hadn't felt in a long time. One thing in particular Trina asked us really stuck with me. At one point, she said: "You know, we understand adoption might not be something you anticipated in your life plan. But no matter what happens, think about this: *Are you doing all this because you want to be pregnant, or because you want to be parents?*"

The distinction was complex, and not one we'd ever considered before. The two ideas were intertwined; in our minds, and in our experience, you got pregnant and then you became parents—it was a straight line progression. But Trina and Joe provided a tangible disruption of this idea; they hadn't experienced a full term healthy pregnancy, but were undeniably loving, supportive, wonderful parents.

Still, Olivia and I had a lot to unpack after our meeting. We knew a lot more about the adoption process now, but there were other options to consider: surrogacy, fostering, donor eggs, and so on.

In this chapter, we'll look broadly at what other paths to parenthood look like, how they work, what they cost, and other basic details. The intent is to provide a solid general overview of these options so you and your partner can simply open up a conversation and consider which might be possible for you. After the general overview, there are some guiding questions you and your partner can discuss to jump start the process of unpacking how you feel about them.

That said, the information that follows is a cursory overview only, and not a detailed description of these paths to parenthood, which are complex processes in and of themselves. There are many excellent resources available which cover these topics in depth, from blogs to books to podcasts, all of which are better qualified to give you detailed information. A great place to start is the podcast "Creating a Family," which focuses on adoption, fostering, and infertility with excellent advice on the process and finances as well as the physical and mental aspects of building your family in these ways (see Appendix A for more recommended media).

DONOR EGGS/SPERM/EMBRYO

- *What is it?* Using eggs, sperm, or embryos which have been donated by verified, healthy individuals. This can be helpful for couples in which one partner has either sperm or egg quality issues, or if for some reason (such as genetic carrier status), you and your partner have difficulty creating genetically normal embryos.
- *How does it work?* Most often, your fertility clinic guides you through the process, often via a third party company or "donor bank" specializing in providing donor sperm, eggs, or embryos. The banks do the work of carefully vetting donors based on their medical history to ensure that the sperm, eggs, or embryos provided are healthy. The donated "items" are then sent directly and safely to your clinic for use. Clinics and donor banks

typically work together on an established basis to ensure compatibility and reliability. If you're considering using donor anything, ensure your clinic and the donor bank have a well-established and trusted partnership.

- *What are the options?* The biggest option you face is choosing a particular donor. Of course, any personalized information is removed here—you won't know your donor's identity and they will not know yours. You and your partner will likely be presented with a binder or website containing various donor profiles with general information like race, height, hair color, eye color, blood type, religious background, educational background, and physical description.
- *What does it cost?* As of 2022, donor sperm is the least expensive, generally costing around $1000 per vial (one vial can be used for one round of IVF of IUI). For donor eggs, you can expect to pay anywhere from $10,000 to $40,000 for a batch (the high cost reflects the price of IVF drugs). And for donor embryos, you may pay anywhere from $3,000 to $15,000 per embryo.
- *Note: All cost estimates in this section are based on a variety of publicly available sources and accurate as of 2022. Costs vary widely based on many factors such as location, agency, clinic, etc.*
- *Anything else to know?* This can be a great option if it's important to you and your partner to give experiencing pregnancy your best shot.

SURROGACY

- *What is it?* Another woman, called the "surrogate", carries a baby for you and your partner, which can be from a transferred embryo (yours or donated), or by your surrogate doing IVF and then using your sperm (or donated sperm) and her eggs.

- *How does it work?* If using your surrogate's eggs, the surrogate goes through IVF, then embryos are grown in the lab and the best is transferred back to the surrogate. If using embryos that already exist, they can be transferred directly to your surrogate.
- *What are the options?* The biggest option here is whether you use your own embryos or use the surrogate's eggs and your sperm (or donated sperm). This is determined by your particular situation. The second major option is to find a surrogate, which is usually done through an agency. Depending on where you are and the particular agency, there are many possible choices here, including finding a surrogate close to you, finding one in another state, or potentially even using an international surrogate.
- *What does it cost?* No surprise—the cost varies greatly, but as of 2022, usually runs in the range of $100,000-$150,000 or more.
- *Anything else to know?* A big note here: surrogacy is not legal everywhere. Check into your local laws and regulations to understand what options are available to you.

ADOPTION

- *What is it?* You and your partner adopt (legally become the parents of) a child born to another woman (usually called the "birth parent" or "birth mother").
- *How does it work?* Generally, you'll work with an agency or attorney who specializes in adoption and in matching hopeful parents with expectant mothers. The agency guides you through the many steps in the process, which include paperwork,

procuring evaluations to ensure you and your partner are able to provide a safe and nurturing home environment, finding expectant mothers to match with, legal services including the legal finalization of the adoption, and other services and support.

- *What are the options?* A first major option is whether to pursue domestic or international adoption. A second major option (more applicable if you're pursuing domestic adoption) is whether you prefer an adoption that is "open" or "closed." The basic difference here: in an "open" adoption, you and the child's birth parent work to maintain some degree of contact as the child grows, whereas in a "closed" adoption, you do not maintain contact with the birth parent. Of course, this is a spectrum—in practice, open adoption can vary widely in terms of how much contact is maintained.
- *What does it cost?* You're probably starting to see a pattern: the cost of adoption varies widely. Many factors affect cost, such as the particular agency you work with, whether it's a domestic or international adoption, and so forth. In general, expect an adoption from start to finish to cost anywhere from $20,000-$50,000.
- *Anything else to know?* Adoption is a particularly complex process; I was grateful to connect with Trina and Joe, as on that first night at the coffee shop alone, we spent over two hours discussing the ins and outs of various paths an adoption can take. I strongly recommend looking at books, blogs, and podcasts for further information and explanation of these options, and connecting with an adoption advocacy group in your region if you're ready to learn more.

Fostering

- *What is it?* You and your partner temporarily care for another person's child or children for some period because the birth parents are unable to provide care at that time. The intent is for the child to return to their birth parents when the birth parents are again capable of providing care.
- *How does it work?* You and your partner work with a foster agency to support you in undergoing training and any necessary certifications, assurances, and licensing (requirements vary by area) to become an approved foster parent. Once approved, the agency works to match you with children in need of a foster home.
- *What are the options?* The biggest option here is which agency you work with. You can generally register a preference for age and gender of any children you foster, though placements that match your preference are not always guaranteed.
- *What does it cost?* Fostering is generally inexpensive; the largest cost is generally taking care of requirements such as a home study to become an approved foster parent. This may amount to a few thousand dollars.
- *Anything else to know?* The most critical thing about fostering is that it's always intended as a *temporary* arrangement—the purpose is to provide care for the child until the point at which their birth parent/parents are able to care for them again. While some fostering arrangements do develop into full legal adoptions, adoption is *not* the primary end goal of fostering.

~ ~ ~

Driving home from our meeting with Trina and Joe, Olivia and I had a lot to think through.

"I can't believe they were in our exact position just a few years ago. Their boys were so sweet," I mused.

"I know, they were adorable. I guess I had just never really envisioned what it would be like to adopt children. I assumed I'd never have to, I suppose," she replied.

"What do you think about the whole being pregnant versus being parents thing?" I asked.

I was a little nervous to bring this up. I knew the question was a lot more pertinent to Olivia than to me. I had no clue what it was like to spend your entire life looking ahead to being pregnant and giving birth. But I knew it was an experience she valued.

"I mean," she said slowly, "I have to think it over. I've always pictured being pregnant, having a growing belly, feeling the baby wiggling inside me. It's really hard to imagine not having that. But...if the alternative is not having kids period...I can't even picture our lives without kids."

"I know. And we aren't giving up on that yet," I replied. "We've got our appointment to go back to the fertility clinic. I don't think we'd start working on adoption or any other options unless we feel like we've tried absolutely everything we can to have our own pregnancy."

"Agreed."

The sun was blazing orange, set low in the sky and creeping ever closer to the horizon.

Olivia continued a moment later: "What do you think would be hardest about adoption, or fostering?"

"I'm not sure," I said, mulling it over. "I guess after seeing Trina and Joe, I feel more confident that it's possible to love a kid as a parent whether they share

your genetics or not. I just know it would take time to fully get in that headspace. I think it would be hard to get over not having "our own" children. I know it's possible, but I know it wouldn't happen overnight."

"I know," she replied , "I know. It would be hard. But you know, if nothing else, I do feel more hopeful now. How do you feel?"

I looked over the fields that rolled by as we drove south toward our village and our white house with green shutters. Early summer crops were just beginning to show green sprouts. Hope was something I hadn't felt in a while. But Trina and Joe had shown me that there is more than one path to parenthood.

I reached over from the driver's seat and gave Olivia's hand a quick squeeze. "I feel more hopeful too."

~ ~ ~

Genetics Make a Baby, Love Makes a Parent

Expect it to take some time to sort out your and your partner's feelings toward donor, adoption, or fostering as possible routes to parenthood. Ultimately, you may decide these paths are not right for you, which is an entirely valid decision. If you do consider these options though, you'll be well-equipped to find the support and information you need to pursue them.

I'll end this chapter with one final thought: while genetics—the combination of sperm and eggs—literally make a baby, what makes someone a parent is much more complex and wonderful. Indeed, many of us can think of examples of people who have their own genetic children, but who did not fully live up to the expectations of being a loving parent.

So what really makes a parent? Actions make a parent: being there to give a child a hug when they scrape their knee. Words make a parent: reminding a child that they are capable, kind, smart, and loved. Choices make a parent: giving a child the rest of your ice cream cone when she drops hers. In short, the choice to provide unconditional care, guidance, support, advice, protection, and time to a child makes someone a parent, regardless of what genetic relationship they do or do not have with the child. Anyone who provides a child with unconditional love is truly acting as a parent, and deserving of that title.

If one of the options described in this chapter ends up being your path to parenthood, remember this: genetics make a baby, but love makes a parent.

CHAPTER 9

WHEN THINGS GO RIGHT: PREGNANCY AFTER INFERTILITY

On a typical Saturday morning at 8:30, we would have been sitting down to a nice weekend breakfast. Perhaps some scrambled eggs, toast, a large cup of coffee for me, and breakfast tea for Olivia.

But this wasn't a typical Saturday. By 8:30 we were already in the checkout line at one of our favorite supermarkets, having plotted out meals and collected all of our usual staples. In fact, we'd been the first customers in the door when they opened at 8:00. A short time later, we were again the first ones present opening up another favorite spot—our town library.

We weren't starting a new resolution to become early birds though—we were up and out at the crack of dawn because it was a big day. It was beta day. Olivia had an appointment for her blood draw at 7:30 am, so on that November Saturday, as the sky gradually lightened out of a dusky haze, we headed to the fertility clinic. Within a few hours, we'd know whether she was pregnant—again.

Ten days prior, the RE implanted an embryo into Olivia for the third time. That transfer day was different from the prior ones in two important ways.

Difference one: it was our first time transferring an embryo on which we had conducted genetic testing. After the second miscarriage, we decided to do another round of IVF to create more embryos, and also to send the embryos out for PGT. So for the first time, we knew we were transferring a genetically tested normal embryo.

The second major difference: for the first time in our three embryo transfers, I was able to be present in the room for the procedure. This wasn't the normal protocol for our clinic; partners generally waited outside during the transfer. But through a combination of our polite persistence in asking for me to be there, and probably some amount of pity from the clinic given all we'd been through, they had agreed.

These two differences gave us a well-needed shot of hope. We knew Olivia could get pregnant, but also now knew we were creating a high percentage of embryos with genetic issues, since genetics most likely caused the first miscarriage, and definitively caused the second. With this obstacle removed, maybe, just maybe this could be our time.

And so we watched the clock, waiting for the library doors to open at 9:00. Usually the clinic called within a couple hours of the beta, so we knew word could come any minute now. Olivia's phone would ring, and there would be our nurse Jennifer on the other line—with news that could change our lives.

Promptly at nine, I saw one of the library staff peer out from inside to scan the parking lot, then reach down and unlock the doors.

"Alright, let's head in," I said. "We can look through the movies and check out a good 80s or 90s comedy. No matter what the news is, we'll have something funny to distract us."

Entering, we veered toward the long stacks of movies available for check out. There would be other times to look for more intellectually stimulating material in our well-stocked library, but this day called for something purely entertaining. I started to think of feel-good movies that could occupy our minds if the news was bad. Maybe something with Leslie Nielsen, or Mike Myers.

Olivia was wandering up another row of the movies when I heard her suddenly rustle in her purse.

"Keegan! They're calling!" she whispered, trying to convey the urgency while respecting the quiet of the library. I rushed around the stack. "What do I do?" she continued, "I've got to take the call, where can I go?"

My head swiveled like an owl, looking for any private cranny we could shunt her into to hear our fate. I zeroed in on an open conference room door along the perimeter. With several large windows facing the library interior, I saw no one was in the room.

"Quick—that conference room—go!" I whispered. Our frantic whispers must have seemed straight out of a Monty Python sketch.

Half-running, half-walking, Olivia hurried toward the room, answering the call on approach to avoid it going to voicemail. I knew Jennifer was on the other line. She wasn't technically even working that morning, but we'd been through so much at that point that she said she'd check our results and call us herself.

I scrutinized Olivia's face, knowing Jennifer would cut to the chase—and that Olivia's reaction would quickly reflect the result.

An agonizing few seconds ensued as I stared into the glass from across the library, looking for any hint of a reaction. Thank goodness it was still early, otherwise other library patrons might be coming up and asking if everything was alright.

And then I saw the smile creep across Olivia's face. A big smile. She brought one hand up and placed it on her upper chest. I made the same half-running, half-walking shuffle toward the conference room. She hung up just as I approached.

I didn't even need to ask what happened. Olivia just smiled and nodded, moisture welling in her eyes, and we wrapped each other in a hug. The transfer had worked. She was pregnant, again.

"The nurse said the beta looks strong," she said after a moment, "and I go back on Monday for the second beta!"

"Well that's great!," I replied.

"I know. Jennifer sounded confident," she added

A few minutes later, movie in hand, we walked out and prepared to call our families to let them know the transfer had worked. At this point in our journey, we had given up on any designs of having a surprise dramatic reveal of a pregnancy.

Olivia looked at me as we approached the car. "How do you feel?"

"Well I'm happy of course..." I started, and then trailed off.

I had to pause and reflect for a moment. It was true, I was happy, but this was our third call from the clinic confirming a pregnancy. I knew this time we had taken different steps by doing the PGT that could hopefully raise our chances of success. But there was no escaping the fact that we'd been pretty traumatized by the two miscarriages. All we had known of pregnancy was of ones that ended in pain.

"I'm happy," I continued, "but I'm anxious too. We know what can go wrong now. I know this is different, and I know we have a good shot. It's just hard not to be worried after what we've been through."

"I know, love," said Olivia. She reached out and squeezed my hand. "I know."

~ ~ ~

Finding out you're expecting can bring a complex mix of emotions to any couple. First, of course there's happiness and hope for the tiny embryo setting up shop. But if you've waited years for this news, endured setbacks, countless visits to doctors, and maybe a whole bunch of shots, you and your partner may experience apprehension, anxiety, or even full on fear about the nine months that lie ahead. Indeed, it's normal even for couples who haven't been through fertility treatment to feel some worries over the course of a pregnancy.

As you can see, I was certainly feeling anxious after we got the phone call in the library confirming we were pregnant again. By this point I knew to expect those feelings, but during our earlier pregnancies, I had been surprised to find that the experience we'd long awaited wasn't all joy and rainbows. I found myself talking to other couples, reading various blogs, and listening to podcasts to learn more about the experience of pregnancy after going through fertility treatment.

What did I learn? First, I learned that pregnancy after infertility can present its own set of mental challenges. Given the pain infertility causes, this is no surprise.

Second, I learned that just as with all the other things you may be feeling discussed thus far, those feelings of worry were quite normal. Understanding what to expect was a big help, and allowed me to think back on other strategies I'd used to care for myself and Olivia in prior parts of our journey, while also responding with some patience when new challenges arose during pregnancy.

Before we dive in, I recognize you may be hesitant to even read this chapter depending on what point you're in on our journey. There were times when we didn't really want to hear anything about pregnancy whatsoever, as we so often wondered if a healthy pregnancy was something we'd ever experience. If you're feeling that way, by all means skip this chapter and come back another time.

Pregnancy After Infertility: Living on the Edge

Being pregnant after infertility can feel as if you're constantly pulled between hope and fear. While I wanted to look forward and think about the good things to come, I felt dogged by the trauma of all we had been through. Even as our third pregnancy progressed, I still found myself saying and thinking things like "*If* we become parents," or "we'll find out the sex *if* we make it that far." The prospect of simply relaxing and enjoying a pregnancy seemed impossible. There's no better way to illustrate what pregnancy after infertility is like than by sharing a few snippets of our experience. So here we go.

- The Reassurance of Regurgitation

"Keegan, come down here!"

I rushed toward the bathroom, knowing pretty well what I'd find. By now, about 8 weeks into pregnancy, we were in a nightly routine. I'd brush my teeth and head to bed to read, and a few minutes later (at least on most nights), I'd hear a heaving hacking sound, followed by Olivia calling my name. Morning sickness had taken full effect, except we had learned that "morning" sickness was in fact a misnomer. Her throwing up never actually struck in the morning—it always came just before bed.

I found Olivia doubled over, sitting on a chair. In what had become a strangely normal routine, I grabbed a plastic grocery bag from the cabinet and held it open while she heaved out some amount of our dinner. I tied up the bag, then headed downstairs and tossed it in the trash while she finished getting ready for bed.

*Even stranger than this having become a nightly ritual, I had to admit that the "evening" sickness was, in a way, a real comfort. With no other day-to-day assurance of the pregnancy continuing, her throwing up was a reminder that…well…*something *was happening. I'd have felt like a terrible husband but for the fact that Olivia also admitted feeling reassured by her nightly nausea.*

Finished with her routine, she came down the hallway and into the bedroom.

"Ugh…how much longer is this going to go on? I mean I know women who throw up every day until giving birth. I don't know if I can make it through that."

"I feel guilty admitting it," I said, "but I'm ok with you throwing up for a few more weeks."

Olivia gave me the eye. "I know it's reassuring, but it's been four nights in a row now. And the only food that doesn't make me gag is plain chicken breast, rice, and pasta. But I also don't want to complain about it and seem ungrateful. We've worked for this for years."

It was certainly a strange spot to be in. But deep down, I really was ok with her throwing up every night for a few more weeks, at least until the next ultrasound at 12 weeks. Maybe that made me a bad husband, but I couldn't help but cling to any possible sign of reassurance that the pregnancy was OK!

- Scanxiety

Another weekday morning, another OB waiting room, and another round of endless and silly commercials about different ailments. We'd already heard ads offering pills to treat several apparently distinct and different varieties of irritable bowel syndrome.

After our awful experience with the ultrasound at the end of our second pregnancy, I resolved further to attend all—or as many as humanly possible—of Olivia's OB appointments if we got pregnant again. Fortunately, here we were. But this was a big one—the twelve week ultrasound. This was the appointment where everything went wrong last time. As if the IBS commercials weren't enough to make our stomach turn already, we had already been nervously anticipating this day since we'd graduated from the IVF clinic (again) three weeks prior.

The sense of deja vu was broken up by one thing—we were at a different OB clinic. The brusque ultrasound tech at our bad appointment left an understandable bad taste in our mouth, so we had asked our IVF doctor if she had any recommendations for OBs who were particularly sensitive and mindful for cases like ours where we'd been through infertility and losses. She offered a few names, and we did some research online, which had led us to this waiting room. Olivia had an establishing appointment with the new OB before even getting pregnant for the third time, but it was a world of difference.

The new OB was extremely sympathetic, patient, and said he would be happy to offer any additional testing or ultrasounds to help ease our minds. After the prior OB who simply emphasized how we were "considered a normal pregnancy" after all we'd been through, this new doctor was exactly what we'd hoped for. Asking our RE for advice had really paid off.

All of this was comforting, but our stomachs were still tied in knots as another round of commercials (this one previewing the day's soap opera episodes) finished up. We had been through the requisite ultrasounds at the IVF clinic, and all looked good, but I couldn't stop replaying our awful ultrasound from the second pregnancy in the days leading up to this one. The seconds stretched interminably. I couldn't help but wonder—what will we be feeling in an hour? Relief? Sorrow, hopes dashed again?

"Olivia?" called a nurse, opening up the door to the clinical area.

I was already clutching her hand, but gave it three quick squeezes as we went back. After the nurse did the typical height, weight, and blood pressure routine, the OB knocked and came in surprisingly quickly. I was grateful not to extend the wait any further.

"Hi, Olivia. It's good to see you again," he opened, "and you must be Keegan. It's nice to meet you."

I understood why she liked the OB straightaway. He was kind, warm, and gentle.

"I'm happy to hear you're pregnant again, and it sounds like everything has gone well thus far at the fertility clinic. You know, the doctor there and I were residents together. She's wonderful. So today we're going to do a couple of things and it shouldn't take too long—first, there's some blood work, next we'll bring out the doppler to listen to the baby's heart rate, and then we'll get you on your way."

Olivia and I glanced at each other—what about an ultrasound? After all we'd been through, simply using the doppler to listen to a heartbeat wasn't enough to give us peace of mind. We'd also heard that the heartbeat can be hard to find at twelve weeks, and had no interest in sitting for agonizing minutes as the doctor tried to pinpoint a tiny heartbeat. It felt a bit ironic to ask for an extra ultrasound when they'd been the source of so much sorrow, but there was no substitute for being able to visualize that growing baby.

"Wait," Olivia interjected. "Can we do an ultrasound—not just a doppler?"

The doctor raised his eyebrows—but it wasn't a look of surprise. It almost seemed as if he was remembering something, perhaps their prior appointment.

"Why of course," he said. "I'm sorry, I know you've been through a lot. And I get it—you want that reassurance. Let's not wait then—we can do the blood work and other things later. The ultrasound is this way, I'll do it myself—follow me."

My heart rate, already elevated, now skyrocketed. The moment of truth was coming. I grabbed Olivia's hand and we followed him down the hallway and into a large room. The ultrasound machine loomed in a corner.

- Can We Connect Yet?

We walked out of the OB a half hour later, smiles on our faces. Within a second of the doctor placing the ultrasound transponder on Olivia's abdomen, we saw our tiny alien-like baby kicking its legs back and forth, heartbeat flickering away.

"I just can't believe it," she said, shaking her head, "I was so nervous. But there it is!"

We had taken a video of the ultrasound, and were now watching it over and over again in the parking lot of the doctor's office.

"Thank goodness we got the referral to this doctor. He's great," I added.

After watching the ultrasound video about thirty more times, I finally started up the car and commenced the drive home.

Turning out of the parking lot, Olivia looked over at me. "So what does this mean in terms of telling people about the pregnancy?"

Despite being twelve weeks along, we had only told our immediate family about the pregnancy. Sharing the news beyond them just seemed too risky. Given our history, the first twelve weeks simply felt like standing on quicksand, always ready to shift underneath us.

I thought about her question. "I know this sounds crazy, but I'm still not sure about sharing. I mean I know we just saw the baby, it looks great, the OB is really happy with progress, but I just can't shake that feeling that something could always go wrong. Am I nuts?"

"No, no," she replied, looking down at her hands in her lap. "I know what you mean. I am happy, I mean this is a big milestone. But it's hard to shake that feeling of worry after all we've been through. Are we going to feel this way through the whole pregnancy if everything continues ok?"

A red light brought our advance toward home to a stop.

I shook my head. "I don't know. I hope not..."

- So When's the Shower?

A few days later, we decided that we didn't want to share the news totally openly yet, but that we'd text and share the pregnancy with a couple of close friends. We figured this was a good balance: it gave us some people who would hopefully help share some excitement, and at the same time, these were the types of very close friends we'd tell anyway if anything were to go wrong. We also knew that one of the couples we were texting had also experienced fertility treatments and pregnancy loss, so we knew they'd be empathetic.

Within a minute of sending texts to the friends, responses came in.

"So happy for you!"

"We've been hoping so much for good news and thinking of you—you guys deserve it! We're thrilled."

*"*String of heart emojis*"*

Despite my initial hesitance to share the news, it was great to hear these reactions. In a way, their joy and excitement gave me a little bit of permission to feel some of the joy and excitement I'd been suppressing in fear of something going wrong.

Olivia and I looked at each other—I knew my eyes were a little misty, and could see tears welling in her eyes too.

"It's not exactly what we expected," she said, "but at least this is some sort of celebratory announcement. I wasn't sure if we'd ever get to do this."

Then our phones buzzed again.

"So have you thought about a baby shower?" read the text message.

Our happy tears quickly changed to looks of exasperation. The answer was YES, we had thought of a baby shower, probably thousands of times, over the prior three years. But we knew responding affirmatively could lead to a barrage of questions we really didn't want to think about yet: Where might the shower be? Do you have any dates in mind? Will it be co-ed or just women? Have you started a registry yet?

Those were all questions that Olivia and I were a little afraid to discuss in any detail. Strange as it was, putting any certainty around plans for a baby shower felt like a line we just weren't ready to cross. It felt presumptuous. It felt like we were placing certainty on having a baby, which even at just over twelve weeks pregnant, didn't feel certain to us. And it felt risky, like maybe we'd "jinx" something by being too confident.

"Ugh," she groaned. "I don't know what to say to this. I know people are going to start asking, but I'm not sure I'm ready to talk about a shower yet."

"Sometimes I wish we could crawl under a rock, come out in a few months, and then just say 'Hey everyone, look, we had a baby,'" I added.

"I know," said Olivia. "It's just hard to connect yet. I want to connect with the baby, I know it's in there from seeing it on the ultrasound the other day, but it still doesn't feel real sometimes. The span from here to actually having a baby in our arms still feels so long. And then I feel guilty sometimes, like I'm not enjoying this as much as I'm supposed to be."

"Well, how about this," I went on, "let's just respond that we haven't thought about a shower yet, but will let them know when we do. It's not exactly the truth, but it's true enough. At least it will stem questions for now."

- The Hiccup Tizzy

Olivia's evening barfing did eventually fade away, right about the time of our twelve week ultrasound. While the following eight weeks were still nerve wracking, it was right around twenty weeks pregnant that a real reassurance came: she felt the baby move. Finally, we had some indicator outside of a monthly ultrasound to provide some sense of what was going on inside her body—and that the little baby in there was well and kicking.

About the same time as she felt the baby move, she started to feel rhythmic taps coming from inside a few times each day. A quick canvas of female friends who had been pregnant told us this was probably the baby hiccuping.

"Wow," I exclaimed, "hiccups! So advanced."

I quickly turned to the internet and searched for information about babies hiccuping in the womb. The first search result told me that it was indeed common for growing babies in the womb to hiccup and for women to feel the hiccups around the same time they start to feel the baby move.

Then, I clicked on the second search result. A quick scan of the first few paragraphs simply revealed the same information I had already read. The next subheading caught my eye, though: "When Can Hiccups Indicate a Problem." My anxious mind whizzed into gear. I read through, my pulse quickening.

"Wait," I mumbled, glancing at her worriedly. "This article says excessive hiccuping can indicate…possible breathing problems? The umbilical cord being wrapped around the neck? Crap!"

Olivia narrowed her eyes. "It says that? About hiccuping? Are you sure?"

She always had a better sense of how to avoid internet-induced anxiety than I did, but it was too late. I was in full-out worry mode, brought right back to our pregnancy losses and panicking about the possibility of coming so far in this pregnancy and then having something terrible happen.

"I mean, that's what this article says. Right here. We'd better call the OB first thing tomorrow morning. Maybe we should even call their emergency line right now!"

Olivia had taken the article and was reading it.

"I can see it says that lower down, but did you see the beginning? Where it says that in almost all cases, hiccups in a baby are totally normal? And that it indicates proper development of muscles involved in breathing? Plus, all the friends I just texted about it said their kids hiccuped in the womb too. Heather

says her daughter hiccuped almost nonstop, and she's a healthy normal five year old now."

Olivia made a special point to tell me every time she felt the baby wiggling over the next few days, especially after hiccups. I had to admit she was right, but I couldn't shake some residual worry. We'd been hopeful in our other pregnancies too, but it just seemed like danger and worry were always lurking.

~ ~ ~

"Today we are Pregnant"

As it turned out, lots of hiccups are almost always nothing to be concerned about. I eventually calmed down and added it to our running list of questions to ask the OB at our next appointment (a great and helpful tactic—keeping a question list!). Indeed, the OB reassured us (or more accurately, me) that the hiccups were utterly normal. But I hope the stories above illustrate what a crazy swing of emotions pregnancy after infertility can bring, as well as some tactics to help manage that time.

As the pregnancy went on, things did gradually get easier. I was able to envision and talk more about a future with a baby in our arms, even though it never felt 100% natural. One piece of advice we heard that was quite helpful was to focus as much as possible on the present moment and day by saying or thinking "today we are pregnant," or even "in this minute, I am/we are pregnant." It's easier said than done of course, but some days, Olivia and I would use this as a mini type of mantra, just saying it to remind ourselves to take the pregnancy one day and one moment at a time without getting caught up in various worries.

I hope above all that your journey results in a healthy pregnancy, and hope you and your partner give yourself space to feel some of the joy if you get the positive beta call.

Indeed, you might find none of this chapter applies to you, and you and your partner simply get pregnant and enjoy the nine months. But if you do get pregnant and find some anxieties creeping in, know it's entirely normal. And if that does happen, I hope these ideas help you feel less alone and more capable of experiencing your pregnancy with presence and strength.

AFTERWORD

THE JOURNEY NEVER TRULY ENDS

A swarm of spidermen, ninjas, and princesses once again scurried up and down our block. Halloween night had arrived again in our little Victorian village. It was three years from the day of our first positive pregnancy test—the one I'd celebrated prematurely.

So much had changed in those three years. Our tree-lined street had changed: we'd now been around long enough to witness the inexorable hand off of homes as families grew and sought bigger houses, and the older generation downsized, or moved closer to children and grandchildren, or passed away.

The entire world had changed, too. The arrival of a global pandemic meant everyone we saw wore a mask, whether part of a costume or simply for their own protection.

Olivia and I had changed too. We'd been stretched to our limits and experienced some of the most difficult lows of our lives. But we also felt stronger than ever, surprising ourselves at how resilient we were. We also felt truly part of the community after several years in town, and looked forward to greeting many of the revelers by name.

And there was one more change. The year prior, in the pre-dawn hours of a July morning, on the hottest day of the year, our daughter Eliza came blazing into the world with a loud wail and one little fist positioned in the air. Needless to say, she was not the only one crying.

"Keegan, get the camera and a few records!" Olivia called. "Let's take a few pictures then get going!"

I could see some of the very young trick-or-treaters already toddling up the street. Eliza was still too young to really know what was going on, but her 60s hippie costume, complete with multi-colored crocheted blanket, crocheted patch dress, a model VW van we'd found, and a copy of Magical Mystery Tour *on vinyl to complete the psychedelic accessories, looked fantastic. Olivia has always been a major Halloween fan, and I was unsurprised to see her set a very high bar on Eliza's first costume.*

We plopped her in a red wagon, arranged her 60s paraphernalia, and set off. It was a slow trip down the street as we paused to greet neighbors and friends. It was an unseasonably warm Halloween evening, and crowds were growing already. Squeals of delight from young ones seeing candy plop in their bags mixed with rustles of leaves crunching underfoot.

"Let's swing by Helen's house before it gets dark," I suggested. Helen was a dear older woman who lived around the corner. She delighted in seeing Eliza, and was a sort of surrogate grandmother figure for all three of us, always ready with a warm smile, kind words, and assurances that she was "saying prayers for us!"

We stepped up on Helen's front porch and knocked. Helen was in her mid-80s, and it always took a few moments for her to get up from her chair and make it to the door. As soon as she saw it was us, she instantly grinned.

"Look at the dear little hippie!" Helen beamed. "She is just the cutest thing. You know, I was too old to be a hippie, even in the 60s. Can you believe that? Talk about an old lady!"

Helen produced a metal bowl from behind her back and stretched it forward. Eliza's eyes widened as she swung her tiny hand and pointed at the bright wrappers. Her excitement and insistence had us breaking into belly laughs.

"No candy for her quite yet," I said, "but she'll be glad to raid your candy next year, Helen."

"Oh for goodness sake," Helen replied, jokingly shaking a finger at me. "One piece couldn't do any harm could it?"

"I know, I know," Olivia jumped in, "you're always giving us treats, Helen! We promise—she'll stick her hand right in your candy bowl next year."

"Well, alright, alright," Helen croaked, feigning disappointment, yet still retaining the glint in her eye. "In that case, I suppose Mom and Dad could use a little sugar for some energy, right? There are no rules against that, I hope?"

She slipped a few mini chocolate bars toward us, which we happily accepted.

"And maybe there will be something else to look forward to next year," Helen continued, "maybe this sweet little girl will have a little brother or sister to join her?"

Olivia and I exchanged glances.

"Well, we sure hope so," I said, half-smiling.

"You know we can't guarantee anything, Helen, but we'll try," she added.

Helen's eyes glimmered. "Well you know I'll be praying for it. Now get out there you three, you've got more houses to visit, and I'm an old lady who needs to put my feet up. Goodbye, dear hearts, and see you soon!"

We turned around and wheeled the big red wagon back toward the corner.

"Helen's so sweet. We're lucky to have her for a neighbor," said Olivia, a sentiment we had expressed many times before.

"She's the best," I replied. "I hope she's right about a little brother or sister. I just hope she's right."

We rounded the corner and looked at the swelling number of families lining the street. I felt immeasurably grateful for Eliza and our little family. But I also knew we wanted more children, and eventually we'd have to return to shots and early mornings at the clinic.

The broad maple branches lining the streets clung to their last handfuls of crumpled leaves as the final rays of sun faded behind them. We kept moving.

~ ~ ~

We feel incredibly fortunate each and every day to have Eliza. As common as infertility is, most people will never know how hard it is to fight for something so basic and fundamental to life as having a child of your own.

Yet after her birth, I sometimes reflected and wondered: Does having her mean…we're not infertile anymore? Does it mean our journey is over? Well, yes and no. It wouldn't be infertility if there were a straight answer, right?

On one hand, we got what we so dearly wanted, and Eliza's existence is a miracle that brings us joy beyond measure. We spent years wondering if we'd ever have any children, so even if we never had another, we know she is more than enough. In this way, some parts of the journey do feel over, and the depths of sadness and emptiness we felt before Eliza seem impossibly distant.

But on the other hand, Olivia and I would love to have another child. As Helen's musings reminded us, achieving this goal means returning to the infertility yo-yo, whether we like it or not. After Eliza's birth, many people told us "watch, now after all that to get her, you'll just get pregnant on your own." It's a pretty thought, but we know the reality. Having a second child means back to blood work, back to shots, and back to planning. And even then, nothing is guaranteed. Perhaps Eliza's birth was just an incredibly fortunate, perfect combination of biology that we had waited years for and couldn't repeat.

Indeed, there are times when I think we're crazy to even consider going back for further IVF treatment. We could simply declare our family-building journey over and spare ourselves months of uncertainty and stress waiting on blood work and counting the days of the two week wait. Yet as attractive as that option seems some days, deep down I know we have to move forward and at least give baby number two a shot. Even if that means, well...giving some shots.

Everyone's family plans are different, but as we reach the point of planning for (hopefully) child number two, I've come to realize that infertility is a journey that never truly ends. And I think I'm at peace with this, or at least I'm at peace with the fact that trying for another baby means accepting the anxiety, uncertainty, and the possible heartbreak that might come with it. There's no guarantee of success, but yet...we move forward.

Indeed, that total lack of guaranteed success is the hardest part of infertility. I wish I could end the book by promising you that if you just keep trying, a baby will come your way. I wish I could promise that if you have a low sperm count, a doctor can surely extract some good sperm via biopsy and solve the issue. I wish I could promise that your first IUI will be a success, or that your IVF round will result in several healthy embryos, or that your next IVF transfer will certainly implant.

No one can promise any of those things.

But I *can* tell you this with certainty: if you communicate openly with your partner, if you work to connect with even just a handful of trusted people to share what you're going through, and if you commit to taking actions that help you get in touch with what you're feeling and support yourself, you can get to the other side of infertility (whatever that looks like for you) and be a stronger person. It's not easy. But you can do it.

So as we draw to a close, I'll repeat my request from the opening: please reach out. I was serious at the beginning when I said I'd love to hear from you with messages on Instagram @theIVFdad, or to TheIVFDad@gmail.com. I personally check and respond to any messages there and would love to hear about your journey, your feedback, your thoughts on this book, or just hear how you're doing.

And remember: you're not alone. Keep moving forward.

Appendix A

Recommended Media (as of 2022)

Books

- Taking Charge of Your Fertility, by Toni Wechsler
- Transcending Infertility, by Dr. Maria Rothenburger

Podcasts

- Infertile AF
- Beat Infertility
- IVFML
- Matt and Doree's Eggcellent Adventure
- Men's Helpline
- Miracles Happen Fertility Podcast
- BFN
- Creating a Family

Movies and Documentaries

- One More Shot
- The Easy Bit

APPENDIX B

TERMS AND ACRONYMS

This is just a basic list of terms and acronyms related to fertility treatments—for a more comprehensive list, see Resolve's great list at https://resolve.org/infertility-101/infertility-faq/infertility-acronyms/.

IUI: Intrauterine insemination, a/k/a the "turkey baster" method. This is where semen is injected directly into the uterus to increase the number of sperm that are present when the egg is released, and as such increase the chance of conception. Often your partner may also take some medications to ensure best conditions for conception, and to ensure the timing of her ovulation.

HCG: Human chorionic gonadotropin. This is the hormone detected by pregnancy tests. The level of HCG in a woman's blood rises rapidly when pregnant.

IVF: In vitro fertilization. This refers, generally speaking, to the entire process of extracting eggs from a woman, mixing the eggs with sperm outside the body in a lab, and then growing the embryos outside the body for several days before transferring them back to the uterus to give the opportunity for implantation.

ICSI: Intracytoplasmic sperm injection. This is a process wherein the laboratory injects a sperm directly into an egg. This can help if for some reason you and your partner's sperm and eggs have difficulty actually carrying out fertilization.

LH: Luteinizing hormone, which is the hormone that rises during ovulation. LH test strips detect this hormone and can help couples time intercourse for the best chance of conception.

ART: Assisted reproductive technology—basically, a catch-all term for any of the technologies like IVF or IUI that we're discussing.

FSH: Follicle stimulating hormone, which is responsible for growing follicles (the sacs that hold eggs) and letting the ovaries know when to start ovulating. A higher level can indicate fewer eggs.

E2: Estrogen, another hormone that testing for your partner will look at. Estrogen is important for many reasons, so

AMH: Anti-Mullerian hormone, which helps provide an estimate of a woman's egg reserves. It naturally diminishes over time, but a doctor will be able to assess whether your partner's AMH level is normal for her age. A lower level may mean a lower egg reserve.

DOR: Diminished Ovarian Reserve. If tests such as AMH and FSH suggest that your partner's egg count is lower than normal, you may receive this diagnosis.

HSG: Hysterosalpingogram. This is an ultrasound-aided test in which the provider shoots a saline solution into your partner's uterus and fallopian tubes to check the shape and for any potential abnormalities.

OHSS: Ovarian hyperstimulation syndrome. During the phase of IVF when your partner is taking medications to stimulate egg growth, there is a risk of over stimulation.

This can cause OHSS, which is basically saying the ovaries have been over stimulated and are growing many eggs very rapidly. OHSS can be quite painful, and is dangerous in extreme cases.

PGD/PGT: Pre-implantation genetic diagnosis or testing. This is a process of sending a very small biopsied piece of an embryo out after it is generated in IVF and before it is implanted back in your partner to assess whether the embryo is made up of genetically normal cells. Identifying and transferring genetically normal embryos can increase the chances of success.

ET/FET: Embryo transfer or frozen embryo transfer. Refers to the procedure of transferring the embryo back into the woman's uterus for hopeful implantation. "Frozen" refers to the embryo, so an FET uses a frozen embryo that has been thawed, whereas an ET uses a "fresh" embryo.

PCOS: Polycystic ovarian syndrome, which is a hormonal disorder that causes enlarged ovaries with cysts. This can cause a range of symptoms and can make it harder to conceive.

TTC: Trying to conceive. I include this just because it may be used in media—as in "We're TTC!"

RPL: Recurrent pregnancy loss. A diagnosis wherein the woman can get pregnant, but has recurrent miscarriages or later pregnancy losses.

US: Ultrasound. Pretty self explanatory!

ACKNOWLEDGMENTS

Inestimable gratitude to the following individuals without whom The IVF Dad would not be here:

- Daniel J. Stone for wise counsel, keen editing, and invaluable encouragement.
- Ian Barton for truly beautiful design work.
- Dr. Maria Rothenburger for sage advice and support.

Made in the USA
Las Vegas, NV
08 July 2022

51274651R00115